PRAISE FOR
CONQUER LIFE'S FRONTIERS

No matter how much fame, fortune, or notoriety we attain, we have failed if we're not pursuing our passion and living out our calling and destiny. Spero T. Lappas will take you on a journey of discovery that will lead you to where you are meant to be and who you are meant to become.

> Jim Stovall, bestselling author,
> *The Ultimate Gift*

When I started reading Dr. Spero T. Lappas' book, I was reminded of author Ben Sweetland's statement, "Life is a journey and not a destination."

We all have great ideas, but as Dr. Lappas points out, it is the action that brings results from those ideas. *Conquer Life's Frontiers* is a guide to a better life. I encourage you to read this book, and I promise: You will treasure what you learn as you read.

> Don Green, Executive Director,
> The Napoleon Hill Foundation; author of
> *Everything I Know About Success*
> *I Learned From Napoleon Hill*

If you're ready to take control, shake off the past, and live the life you've always dreamed of, *Conquer Life's Frontiers* will show you the way.

Greg S. Reid, bestselling author of
Stickability and co-author of
Three Feet From Gold

In *Conquer Life's Frontiers*, Dr. Spero Lappas teaches us how to create our personal Renaissance as if it were a work of art. No wonder! He walked away from a career of position, prestige, and power in order to find a deeper and more meaningful form of success. What are you doing with your life right now? It doesn't matter if you dig ditches, compose symphonies, or save lives. *Conquer Life's Frontiers* will show you how to discover and embrace your True Self. This book should be required reading for every man and every woman who wants to learn how to blaze a personal trail to individual fulfillment.

Mitzi Lee Trostle,
Public Media Senior Executive;
Nonprofit Development Expert

Revolutionary life-change almost always requires a catalyst to send us out of our comfort zone and toward the life we envision. *Conquer Life's Frontiers* is that catalyst and Spero T. Lappas is the guide who shows us the way.

Don Hummer, Ph.D.
Author; Professor, Penn State University

CONQUER LIFE'S FRONTIERS

A Philosophy of Individual Fulfillment

*Create a Personal Renaissance
at Any Moment—
Even Now*

SPERO T. LAPPAS, PhD
FOREWORD BY DR. CHARLES KUPFER

ALITHOS

Alithos Media Group, LLC
P.O. Box 6065
Harrisburg, PA 17112

ISBN: 978-0-692-87919-1

LCCN: 2017941955

DEDICATION

"Fortune favors the bold."
PLINY THE ELDER

This book is dedicated to you, the reader who summons the courage to trade forfeit for fulfillment. Enjoy your journey across Life's Frontier to your own Personal Renaissance.

Table of Contents

PART THREE — PERIL

PART FOUR — ESSENCE

PART FIVE — EPILOGUE

FOREWORD

Knowledge is precious, but if we don't know what to do with it—how to use it, how to put it to work for ourselves and the world around us—its benefits are abstract at best. True scholars and teachers know this. They have to be learned, steeped in their subjects, capable of understanding ideas great and small. But they also have to help us grasp the subject and apply it to our lives. Spero Lappas is that kind of scholar and teacher. His book, *Conquer Life's Frontiers*, is the all-too-rare work that takes the most important thoughts of the greatest thinkers and presents them in ways that can change our lives.

Ranging far and wide, from ancient Greece to the American frontier, from the top of Mount Everest to the deepest recesses of the human spirit, Lappas takes us on a tour of thoughts and actions; thoughts with true power to change our world, and actions that help us ensure those changes are changes for the best. But Lappas does much more than merely impress us with his scholarly knowledge. In fact, this book is not about him at all. It is about us. Like the best teachers since Socrates questioned pupils at the Agora, Lappas challenges and inspires us, giving us an inestimably precious gift: specific lessons on how to put the mighty ideas he marshals to work so that we can live more directed, courageous, fulfilling lives.

Whether he is showing us how Norse mythology points the way to our Personal Renaissance, or explaining how to dodge the arrows shot by those who wish to thwart us, Lappas is relentless in his insistence that a better life is not simply something we should dream about, but something we can—we *must!*—achieve. I have yet to read a more humane, relevant, supportive, or trenchant volume so suitable for the person struggling to find the best pathway through life's thickets to that place we all dream of in our hearts. Lappas shows us, step by step, with concrete and easily followed directions, how to discern our path, how to listen to our best selves, how to gain from the finest advice from the greatest thinkers and doers of the last three thousand years, and ultimately, how to live the lives we were put here to live. Like the figures whose lessons he gives us, Lappas is concerned throughout with helping readers gain from the lessons he and his fellow philosophers and action-masters know so well. *Conquer Life's Frontiers* is more than a self-help book. It is a guide to a better life.

Dr. Charles Kupfer
March 2017

Dr. Kupfer is associate professor of American studies and history at the Pennsylvania State University and the author of *Indomitable Will: Turning Defeat into Victory from Pearl Harbor to Midway.*

AUTHOR'S NOTE

Throughout this book, I often recount actual events that illustrate my points or that are historically relevant to the events that I describe. In the interest of privacy, I have changed the names of the people and of many of the places involved in these accounts. One exception is the name of the restaurant in chapter 14, which, for reasons that will become obvious, I call by its true and wonderful name.

*"We have two lives,
and the second one begins when we realize
that we have only one."*

CONFUCIUS

INTRODUCTION

Why I Wrote This Book and Why You Should Read It

On May 29, 1953, a forty-two-year-old New Zealand beekeeper named Edmund Hillary became the first person to reach the summit of Mount Everest. Many men had tried that climb before Hillary. Some lost their fortunes and reputations. Some lost their lives. The challenge of standing on top of the world had inspired passionate ambitions in thousands of famous, and many not so famous, adventurers. The great British mountaineer Sir George Mallory thrilled the world in 1924 when he told a reporter that he would conquer Everest "because it's there," but when he tried it two months later he died on the mountain's northeast ridge. Hillary, never one to speak words that he might later have to swallow, saved his boast for the way down. After leaving the summit, he told his lifelong friend George Lowe, "Well, George, we knocked the bastard off." Yes, they had.

Hillary became an international superstar. *Time* magazine called him one of the most influential persons of the twentieth century. Queen Elizabeth II made him a Knight Commander of the British Empire, and many other countries honored him with their own awards and titles. He landed an airplane on the North Pole, crossed the South Pole on a tractor, and wrote over a dozen books. The Sir Edmund Hillary Himalayan Trust built more than thirty schools, a dozen medical clinics, and two hospitals. It built airfields, bridges, and water pipelines that served remote populations throughout the exotic land of Nepal.

A full and fulfilling life if ever there was one. A brilliant life of adventure, heroism, charity, achievement, and fame. But what did Sir Edmund himself consider to be his greatest accomplishment? Which of his many great feats and achievements did he see as the capstone to a life that inspired a generation? We know the answer to that question because we have the words of his own mouth. "I am a lucky man," he said. "I have had a dream and it has come true, and that is not a thing that happens often to men."

The realization of his dream to climb Everest was the signature achievement of Hillary's life, and it changed everything that followed it. After that, but only after that, he could stand at the North and South Poles, educate generations, restore health to thousands, achieve fame and fortune, break the back of ignorance, cure diseases, save lives, and give hope to whole nations. How did all of that happen? What was it about the humble beekeeper that had changed on the roof of the Himalayas?

We often describe mountaineers as having "conquered" the peaks they climb, but a mountain is nothing more than a geological formation, rock and stone, earth and ice. It has no heart, no spirit, no consciousness. No one can "conquer" such a thing. Neither Hillary nor anyone else bends it to their will or forces it to submit. Hillary did not even claim Everest as British territory. So when he told his friend George that they had "knocked the bastard off," what could he have meant? The mountain stood as tall and proud as ever; Hillary had not changed it by as much as a single pebble. The thing that Hillary had knocked off, the thing he captured and subdued, was not the mountain itself: it was the *dream* of climbing the mountain, his mastery of risk and chance. Mountains don't get conquered, *dreams* get conquered—they are the frontiers of our interior lives. That is why years later, even after so many other great accomplishments, none of those other things mattered as much as the one singular event that took place within the confines of his deepest human spirit. His greatest feat, the thing that does not often happen to human beings but that had indeed happened to him was simply this—he had found a dream he loved and he made it come true.

That kind of dream realization—the conquest of a personal resolve that traverses the frontiers of our imaginative aspirations—is what I call the creation of a *Personal Renaissance.* And even though I have not climbed Mount Everest (yet), I have created a Personal Renaissance of my own.

I know that there are a thousand books out there about changing your life for the better, and many of them promise wonders and miracles. Think positive thoughts. Attract your fortune. Conquer your doubts. Manifest your destiny. If you found this book in a bookstore you probably picked it off a shelf that was filled with titles about reinventing your life, renewing your life, restoring your life, et cetera, et cetera. If I know anything about human nature (and I do), I bet I know what you're thinking: "Why should I listen to this guy? Who is *he* to give *me* advice?"

I get it. Those are fair questions, so let me answer them.

As I will talk about in the chapters of this book, I went from being a successful but unhappy lawyer to becoming a graduate student, and then a PhD recipient, and then a college professor. That was once my dream and I made it come true. I reified my ambition—I took a thought and made it a fact.

At many points during my life, things have been pretty bleak. I have had most of the kinds of problems that any person can have. I grew up so poor that I was embarrassed to have my friends see where I lived. I have been so broke that I couldn't pay my bills. I have been depressed and despondent, in and out of therapy and treatment. My first childhood memory is the fear of homelessness. I once had a deadly disease and did not know if I would live till morning. I have failed at many things and set goals that I didn't achieve. I have made plans that I never reached and aspired to ambitions that never came close to coming true. I have seen my life broken at the strong places and at the weak ones, and I have lived in that dark corner of the soul where it is almost impossible to believe that there is a light out there somewhere, even if it is out of sight.

I have been in that place where you have nothing but a dream and a portfolio of discouragement; I have been in the place where everyone around you thinks you would be crazy to want anything to change because your life seems so perfect already; and I have been in most places in between. I know what it feels like to have a desire and to wonder how you can summon it out of the world of wit and fancy and make it a concrete, real-life part of the world of facts and things. And I know what it feels like to actually make it happen: to materialize the dream.

You may be in a pretty bad place in your own life right now. Or you may be (almost) on top of the world. Either way, you have picked up this book and turned past the cover and started reading it—all of which suggests that you must want things to be different for you. You are no longer satisfied being what you are right now. You want to be something different and better. So did I. Maybe you have an unfulfilled ambition, something that you dream about whenever you are brave enough to dream. You may have already tried wishing, wanting, and goal-setting, but none of it has worked. I hope that after reading this book you understand why it hasn't.

The longing you feel is the same one that I once felt. I took my own longing out of my world of "what ifs" and made it part of my world of "here goes." That was my Personal Renaissance. As for yours, I have no idea what it might look like or what fulfilled dreams will pack it to the brim with satisfaction. It doesn't really matter. You can do the same thing that I did with whatever dream your imagination and audacity allow you to have. Just like Hillary, you can "knock the bastard off." Your own Renaissance dream will arise out of some aspect of the life you are living right now that makes you feel unsatisfied, incomplete, or inauthentic. For me it was work-related, a new career, but yours can be anything at all. It can touch any aspect of your life. Maybe your personal life is unsatisfactory. Maybe it's your relationships, your business, your employment, your health, or your fitness. Do you want a new lifestyle? A bigger house? More money? Your last first date? A championship golf game? Maybe none of those things by themselves or all of them together cause you to feel that your life is out of kilter, off balance. Do you want to climb a real mountain? Bake a better cake? Your resolve for a Personal Renaissance will grow out of that deficiency, and this book will show you how to nurture and reify that resolve.

I wrote this book to share the lessons that I have learned along the way. I've been there. I've done it. And that is why you should read it. If you want to stop accepting an unacceptable existence, then you are ready to conquer your Life's Frontier.

There is a belief afoot in the world today that all you have to do is sit still and wish your way to a brighter future. Many authors sell books about such a belief, and many buyers pay good money to read them. If you agree that wishing and hoping will change your life (they won't), then please answer one simple question for me: Why haven't your fantastic super mind-control powers made your life perfect already? That's what I thought.

In these pages we will talk about developing a resolve that won't be defeated or refused. We will learn how to avoid letting the problem of *The Three Blanks* stop you in your tracks. We will examine why it's a bad idea to place all your eggs in the basket of goal-setting. We will learn about strategy and tactics, and differentiate between the inadequacies of an uncertain future and the rewards of an immediate rebirth. We will travel around the world to ancient and exotic lands and listen to the words of philosophers, adventurers, and great thinkers of every type. We will hear the stories of the ages and consider what they can teach us. We will become explorers of the well-lived life and the practitioners of living it in full.

When I said in the title that this is a book for *any moment*, I meant it. I started my own personal journey when I was already "of a certain age." Maybe you are, too. There is a wonderful poem by Alfred, Lord Tennyson that portrays the great hero Ulysses when, in numbers and in years, he was an old, old man. His physical strength had faded, and his fame had evaporated. Nonetheless, Tennyson describes him as being ready for adventure and eager for new exploration and discoveries. "Come, my friends," commands the hero. "'Tis not too late to seek a newer world." And so it is for you and me. It is not too late for us to seek our newer world. There is something brand-new out there just waiting to be discovered. And it is never too late to start discovering.

On the other hand, some of the oldest people I know are young in years. Maybe you know someone like that or maybe, just maybe, that is *you*. You may be in the full bloom of youth, lithe and beautiful, and not a wrinkle to be seen. Maybe you can run a mile in your sleep and you understand every single social media meme and trope. Yet you may still have attitudes that are old and weary; you may already be losing your spirit of adventure.

As a professor, I have taught many students who seem to have decided at an early age that there were parts of the world of opportunity that were closed to them. There were dreams that were too big for them to grasp. They felt that there was a path set out for them and they dared not stray from that path. They had decided—or more often than that, they believed that it had been decided *for* them—that their course through life was already set down and paved. Their world told them what they *had to be*—a doctor, a lawyer, a businessperson, a teacher, or whatever. Others felt that something in their world had limited their opportunities for them and told them what they *could not be*—they had skipped right over the selection stage of life and moved from a childhood that knew no limits right into a narrowed maturity of tunnel vision and blinders.

Old or young, no one has to limit their future with an unfulfilling vision of their own existence. Young or old, rich or poor, healthy, infirm, educated, uneducated, none of that matters as much as this—are you willing to make this *your* moment?

Are you willing to have a dream and make it come true?

Are you willing to knock that bastard off?

Was Edmund Hillary right?

Would you like to find out?

That's what I thought.

Let's start climbing together.

A Thought Experiment

The Imaginary Train

Imagine that you are a passenger on a speeding train. You are riding in a beautiful carriage, sitting in a comfortable seat right beside the window. You spend your days looking out through the small rectangular window and watch as the world rushes by. The train roars on through cities, fields, and forests. Over rivers and mountains. Onward and onward. Sometimes faster, sometimes slower, but never stopping. You watch the passing scene transfixed as it remains untouchable beyond the glass. Your own reflection, partial and transparent on the window, makes you part of the strange and passing scene. The world beyond is filtered through your image and your identity. You apprehend the reality of the outer frontier as if your individuality were written all over it.

You see the landscape as one fleeting glimmer at a time. Never whole, the world complete in its entirety. You can never revisit the land just passed or the places left behind. You cannot see what's up ahead. You don't know where the train is headed or when it will stop. There is no one you can ask.

You look out past your echoed face, a ghost on the glass.

PART ONE

Renaissance

"This perennial rebirth…the Frontier is productive of individualism."

INTRODUCTION

On October 21, 1892, over 750,000 visitors crammed into the 690 acres between Jackson Park and Midway Plaisance for the opening of the Chicago World's Fair. It was the largest gathering that had ever attended any single event anywhere on earth. The Fair, officially called the World's Columbian Exposition, celebrated the American experience and commemorated the 400th anniversary of Christopher Columbus landing in the New World. Until it closed the following year, the Fair hosted the pavilions of forty-six different countries and boasted 200 buildings. It had one of the largest artificial water pools in history to symbolize Columbus's long sea voyage of discovery. Helen Keller and Alexander Graham Bell were among the scores of dignitaries who attended. Milton Hershey, namesake of the bars and kisses, was there, and he bought a European chocolate-making process that he later put to good use. Thomas Edison and George Westinghouse spent millions of dollars and years of prestige fighting their War of the Currents, direct versus alternating, over the right to illuminate the Exposition (Westinghouse won), and Katherine Lee

Bates was so taken with the sparkling White City section of the Fair that she mentioned it years later when she wrote the fourth stanza of "America the Beautiful" ("Thine alabaster cities gleam, undimmed by human tears!").

The Columbian Exposition featured the world's first Ferris wheel, the first carnival midway, the first mechanized sidewalk, the first commercial movie theater, and a cannon that could shoot a ton of iron over fifteen miles. On July 12, 1893, it also featured a meeting of the American Historical Association. At that meeting, the country's leading historians listened to a speech by a thirty-two year old professor from the University of Wisconsin. He was named Frederick Jackson Turner.

Compared to the monumental amazements that surrounded it at the Exposition, a short talk to a bunch of historians may not seem to be the kind of event that could turn the world upside down. Turner was politely received by the historians, but his ideas did not make much of a splash—at least not at first. In time, however, scholars and experts all around the world recognized Turner as a genius. The speech that proved his genius was called "The Significance of the Frontier in American History."

The young man from Wisconsin introduced the world to the brilliant notion of "The Moving Frontier"—an imaginary, but energetic, boundary line that stretched between the settled land of the early American East and the wild, untamed land of the West. The frontier was a geographical construct, but Turner theorized that it was much more than that. It demarcated the old and the new, the past and the future. It was the conceptual edge of the world we knew and the doorway to the one we didn't. It was the verge one had to cross to leave *that-which-once-was-so* and enter *that-which-still-can-be*. Turner's Frontier Thesis, as his idea came to be known, postulated that the wild uncertainty of a vibrant, unknown future gave birth to the opportunity for every new creation.

The frontier introduced a wild domain where aptitude spawned opportunity, where curiosity combined with courage, and where adversity gave rise to unforeseen potential. Its border was ferociously unclear. Its opacity concealed the dangers beyond its limit, insisting on daring and boldness for the intrepid pioneer. Conquering the frontier required a willingness to embrace mystery, to be glad with occult ambiguity. Turner's frontier traveler had to accept jeopardy and risk. The young professor told his Chicago audience that the frontiersman's task demanded strength combined with acuteness, an inventive turn of mind, a masterful grasp of things, energy, and courage. As compensation for audacious nerve, Turner's threshold to potentiality promised to change the lives of every trailblazer who crossed the line from security into hazard. Everyone who dared to trade settlement for uncertainty would be rebirthed.

Turner knew the same thing that you and I know: that a person, like a country, can become reborn in the audacity of fulfillment. The virtuosity of Turner's idea perfectly fit the theme of the Columbian Exposition, an extravaganza that called itself the beginning of an American Renaissance.

CHAPTER 1

THE RENAISSANCE OF
MY TUSCAN SUMMER

*"When you come to a fork
in the road, take it."*
YOGI BERRA

A lot of people say they can't remember the specific moment when their life began to change. I can. It happened about five years ago in Florence, Italy. In June.

It was a hot summer day, and I had been traveling through Italy with a group of undergraduate art history students. My friend Brianna was their professor, and she had asked me to come along. Brianna is a brilliant art historian, and her invitation to travel with a group of bright students guided by a PhD of Italian art was a great opportunity. Even so, I almost didn't do it. In those days I often blew chances at great opportunities if they would take me too far out of my comfort zone. Looking back at that summer, I am very glad that I didn't blow this one.

We landed in Milan and for three weeks we learned about some of the greatest artistic treasures the world has ever seen.

We viewed fabulous sites in Tivoli, Sienna, Mantua, Venice, and Rome. We studied museums, galleries, architecture, sculpture, and painting. On that particular day in June we toured Florence's magnificent churches and cathedrals. The day was hot and the walk was grueling, so when Brianna gave us a free afternoon I was glad to find an authentic Irish pub a few blocks from my hotel. I opened its heavy wooden door and walked out of the hot sun and into the cool, dark taproom of the Piper's Thumb. I sat at the bar, ordered some bangers and mash, and cooled off with a Harp Lager.

I had just left the Basilica of Santa Maria Novella. One of Florence's greatest attractions, it had taken Italian craftsmen over a hundred years to build before its completion in 1360. It contains eight separate chapels, each filled with artistic masterpieces. *The Nativity* by Botticelli, *The Crucifix* by Brunelleschi, frescoes of the Last Judgment by Nardo di Cione—all of these and more make Santa Maria Novella one of the most beautiful spots in Florence. It stands today as a monument to the historical age that scholars call the Renaissance: a time when the luster and radiance of art, science, and knowledge replaced the gloom and shadows of the era called the Dark Ages.

Renaissance means "rebirth," and it signifies the creation of wisdom and the rejection of confusion. The historical Renaissance started in the 1300s when philosophers and kings uncovered ancient wisdom that had lain buried for ages upon ages, in some cases for thousands of years. Medieval darkness gave way to a modern age that produced Michelangelo and Leonardo da Vinci, Magellan and Columbus, Isaac Newton and William Shakespeare. Renaissance thinking lifted the Western world out of the bleak ignorance of superstition and into the bright light of intelligence, beauty, creativity, exploration, and discovery. The wisdom that erupted out of the darkness reignited humanity's capacity for growth and development.

And it had all started right there in Florence.

That June was a happy time in my life and in the life of my family. Two days before I flew to Italy, my daughter had graduated from college magna cum laude with double majors in philosophy and political science. In the fall, she would begin her studies at one of America's finest law schools. My son would soon defend his doctoral dissertation and earn his PhD in cognitive science. As for me, I was one of Pennsylvania's leading lawyers, and my practice was going great. I had money rolling in, and I was coming off a huge win in a murder case for an innocent eighteen-year-old client. These were the personal and professional bright spots, but there was darkness, too. For me, as for many people, happiness coexisted with dissatisfaction in an emotional demilitarized zone where a shaky peace treaty prevailed. Those were the things I was thinking about on that hot summer day in a shady pub in Florence. I was fifty-eight years old, and I was at a crossroads.

I had practiced law since I was twenty-five, and it was no secret among my colleagues and friends that I was unhappy. The mystery, though, the one question that was hard for them (and for me) to answer, was "Why?" Over the course of thirtyplus years I had earned a terrific reputation. I had taken on cases that no one else dared to touch. I had freed clients who were falsely accused of terrible crimes, and I had handled some of the biggest trials in Pennsylvania. I kept a framed lithograph of an electric chair in my office, and every time I saved a client from the death penalty I glued a gold star to the glass. By that summer it showed ten stars. I had a beautiful corner office at a prominent law firm. I enjoyed the respect of my community, I did important work, and I was good at it. I drove a fancy convertible, and I lived in a big house in a prestigious neighborhood. So what was missing?

That was the question that had dogged me as I wandered around Italy and that occupied me that afternoon in the Piper's Thumb. On the other side of the world, I confronted the fact that stared me in the face every day I woke up at home: I was miserable and I didn't know why. I was stressed out all the time, and I felt like the direction of my own existence was governed by accident and circumstance. My trajectory, my velocity, was beyond my control. I lived with a nagging discontent that often blossomed into a low-grade depression. Therapy hadn't helped. Medication didn't help. Even exciting travel just reminded me of the old saying that no matter how far you go, you can't escape from yourself. My life seemed so perfect from the outside, but inside it was a mess. Should I really go back to it?

Sure, I would go back to Pennsylvania. I wasn't about to stay in Europe and leave my kids behind. But I had to find a way to stop being the hapless passenger in my own life, propelled forward through good and bad situations and tied to the casualty of season. From the safe perspective of 5,000 miles I asked myself, *What should I return to?* I had reached a fork in my road—but at least I had a glimmer of where I wanted it to lead.

I had always known that I loved studying and learning. An afternoon with a good book was one of my greatest pleasures. When my kids were in college and graduate school I enjoyed being in those places with them and soaking up the atmosphere of knowledge and learning. I loved being in a place where those things mattered more than how many cases you won, or how much money you made, or how big your office was. I knew that my happiest future would involve teaching and writing, and I had long dreamed of being a college professor. In fact, I had applied for a few faculty positions in the past, but I was always turned down because I didn't have the kind of advanced degrees that colleges look for. Those rejections showed me that in order to realize my dream I would have to go back to school. Was I really willing to do that? It would mean a complete reorganization of my life and a difficult journey to a totally different lifestyle. I would go from making a lot of money to making none. I would go from being a local big shot, the center of attention whenever I walked into a courtroom, to being just another pupil, an ordinary student in a cohort of ordinary students. I would leave the comfortable lifestyle that I had built with decades of hard work for a new world where everything was strange. I would be entering undiscovered country. Did I have the courage to dare such a trip? Could I be tenacious enough, brave enough, and maybe even reckless enough to allow myself to be reborn into a new identity, a new way of living, a challenging life with uncertain prospects and an obscure future?

Those thoughts swirled inside my head as I glanced up and noticed that one of the other patrons was leaving the pub. After he walked through the door, it seemed to stay open a little bit longer than necessary. The sun was hanging low in the sky, but its light was still brilliant and yellow. It poured through the open door and flooded the cool darkness of the taproom. It was so bright that it blinded me for a moment. When my eyes were able to pierce the glare, I could see the Basilica and Plaza of Maria Novella. I got up and walked out into the busy street. It teemed with tourists and shopkeepers and sightseers and churchgoers. When I crossed the threshold from the shadowy pub into the brilliant sun, I could feel the bustling spirit of twenty-first-century Florence spin around me, but I also felt the quieter spirits from distant centuries past. I breathed in the life of the new and the old and realized that I had been musing about rebirthing my own life in the middle of a city that had once taught the whole world how to be born anew.

Almost a thousand years before, the Renaissance of the world had started right where I was standing. On that steamy afternoon amidst the sunny blaze of summer, my Personal Renaissance started there, too.

A couple weeks later I returned to Pennsylvania, but I did not return to my previous life. I wrapped up my remaining legal cases and I stopped taking new clients. I told the managing partners of my firm that I was giving up my office and leaving the law, and I began referring my clients to other lawyers. Some clients were grateful for the help I had given them already; others were bitter and felt betrayed. I traveled from town to town, courthouse to courthouse, and gave the news to the friends and colleagues with whom I had worked for so many years. Some of their reactions were touching, some were angry. A few of the lawyers and judges thought that I had lost my mind. Others were shocked and could not believe that I could leave the law, and they accused me of turning my back on all of the injustices that still needed to be rectified. I understood those reactions. I had cycled through most of them myself. Some people thought that I was having a mid-life crisis and that my Personal Renaissance was just a different kind of red Corvette and trophy girlfriend. But, to the surprise of more than a few of the smartest people in town, I finished what I started, closed the doors to my law office, figured out how to be admitted to graduate school, and then I did it. Fourteen months later I was sitting in my first graduate school seminar. As I looked around the classroom I realized that it was one of the best moments of my life.

Three years later, I had a PhD in American studies and I was living the academic life that I had dreamed about. I was teaching young people about history, culture, and civilization, but more than that, I was teaching them about life and living and how to shape their futures. I left a closetful of fancy suits on their hangers and went to work in jeans and sweaters. I felt the peace of mind that proved to me that I had made the right decision.

Every day since then has given me the opportunity to open minds and change lives. But only after I had changed my own.

As we set out to conquer life's frontiers, we can use some guideposts along the way. Here is the first one.

FIRST GUIDEPOST

You really can create your own Personal Renaissance.

The Imaginary Train

You sit in your carriage and wonder—what of the train itself? You can see the interior of the car in which you sit, but you never see the outside of the train. What color is it? What company name is written on its side? How many cars, how many windows, how many other faces peering through reflections of themselves? But more than that, what makes the train go? What is the motor of your journey? In what direction does it head? And how far do the tracks reach? When must you get off the train?

Where did you board it?

All of these are good questions, and an experienced traveler would be wise to ask them. But you spend very little of your time wondering about the train or its course. Mostly, you just look out the window and watch the world speed along. An ever-changing panorama made of millions of flashing moments, each one disappearing into a vanishing dissolve of what came last.

One day you notice a switch by the center of the car. "Emergency Stop," it says. There is a smaller sign next to it— "Danger!

Don't touch." You can't understand why you haven't noticed them earlier in your journey. "Emergency Stop"? Stop the train? What would that be like? Would the train crash? Would you survive? Would it be fun? Or scary?

If the train stopped, could you actually get off? And if you did, could you ever get back on it again? Could you make it start again? Or would you be forever stranded someplace strange, on the frontier of a wild uncertainty?

And so, day after day, sunrise after sunrise, you look at the switch that says "Emergency Stop" and you do nothing. Nothing but wonder and ride the train. You stare out the window and watch the world escape your grasp, one immaterial glimpse of present at a time. The ever-fleeting rush and roar of now.

CHAPTER 2

GETTING FROM
"WHY NOT?" TO "OF COURSE!"

"If you board the wrong train,
It is no use running down the corridor
in the other direction."
DIETRICH BONHOEFFER

I am writing this chapter in Mikel's coffee shop right across Venizelos Boulevard from the University of Athens. A light rain has been falling in Athens for the last two days, but today is bright and clear with the Aegean sun. Even in early January, the weather is warm enough for me to stroll through the city in short-sleeves and a light jacket. The neighborhoods that I pass through have names that once seemed strange to me—Thissio, Monasteraki, Syntagma, Omonia, Panapistimio—but now they sound as familiar and ordinary as the streets in my own hometown. Well, they are familiar at any rate. As I learn and relearn every day, no place is truly ordinary.

At 11:00 a.m., this outdoor restaurant is packed. Middle-aged and elderly men huddle around tiny café tables, animated in conversations composed as much of gestures as of words. They swing the loops of beads on a string, *komboloi* or "worry" beads, that are a standard fashion accessory for the Greek male. Women sit in groups of their own, exchanging community news and gossip, sometimes blessing themselves with the sign of the cross to ward off the contagion of any reported illness or (worse yet) infidelity. Younger people sip their frappes and check their phones while laughing more loudly than the older folks appreciate. Pigeons walk and fly amidst the tables. A few minutes ago one of them knocked over some water glasses, smashing them to bits on the cobblestone floor. No one seems to mind. Street peddlers wander through the crowd offering fistfuls of lottery tickets. They only approach the men. I haven't bought one yet. I won't have too many more chances left. I leave Athens in three days.

I have been here for about a month now. Fall semester ended a few weeks ago, and I came to Athens to work on this book. Since I got here, I have learned which markets have the best cheese, which coffee shops are open early and which are open late, and what days the greengrocer on Polopoulo Street has the freshest tomatoes. I have learned about tea made from anise seeds and from sage leaves. Every morning I drink large cups of deep black Greek coffee, which I have learned to order in two languages—"thiplos (a double) medium sweet"—and I know the trick of when to stop sipping it so that you don't get a mouthful of the muddy sludge that lies on the bottom of the cup. I have a favorite bartender at my favorite bar, and he has introduced me to something called raki, a liquor made from fermented figs. He pours it into tall, thin shot glasses, one for each of us, and we toast one another by clinking our glasses together and then banging them on the bar.

I have a tiny apartment with no luxuries and few conveniences. Every morning when I wake up I look out my bedroom window into the kitchen of the bakery that lies directly across the back alley. The baker is a lean young man who always wears a white T-shirt, white pants, and a black beret as he pulls the loaves of crusty bread out of his stone oven with a huge wooden paddle. I buy a loaf every day for seventy cents—"Ena psomi," I say—and then I make my selection by pointing to the shelf where the bread is stacked like cordwood. The bakery's atmosphere is perfumed with cinnamon, clove, and warm honey, and every countertop and table is piled high with trays of powdered cakes and pastries made from sheets of phyllo wrapped around walnuts, pistachio, sugar, and dates. There are twists and braids, baked golden and covered with sesame. The young woman behind the counter wraps my bread in tissue paper before she puts it in the bag. She takes my one-euro coin with a smile and asks for the next customer's order while she gives me my change. She wears a lacy apron and the kind of cap that nurses used to wear in movies from the sixties.

I have memorized the subway map, navigated my way through ports and boat schedules, steamed to an island in the Saronic Gulf, climbed the Acropolis, visited temples to the gods of antiquity, and haggled with street merchants over the price of walnuts. In short, my Greek adventure has made me part of the life of this ancient, modern, untamed, singular land. A small part of it, to be sure, and a temporary one at that, but part of it nonetheless.

All of this started about six weeks ago in the office of the professor who had once been my graduate school academic adviser. Jim and I stayed close after graduation, and we were talking about our plans for the approaching winter break. He would be working from home on his latest project, a book about the history of baseball. I told him I was also writing a book and that I was considering a trip to Athens to work on it, but I was undecided because the trip would be an expensive extravagance in my new life as a poorly paid adjunct professor.

Besides, I didn't have a place to stay, and the Greek economy was sketchy.

Jim looked at me as if I were slightly crazy and shook his head. "Okay," he said. "Those things may be true. Probably are. But you should still go. I mean—*why not?*"

Why not indeed?

As soon as I heard the "Why not?" question I sat back and said, "Of course!" The next day I found an apartment and booked a flight. I came to Greece and found out, much to my delight, that my "Of course!" decision inspired me to better and more productive writing than I had accomplished in many months at home. I wrote in cafés and tavernas, in a library, on a ship, and sometimes I wrote on the small table in my apartment. I wrote some of these pages on jet planes and in the airports of four countries. It is a different book than the one I imagined before I made this trip, and when I finish it after going home (no, I did not write the whole thing in one month!), it will wander across paths that are inspired by the places I visited, the things I saw, and the people I met. All because I conceived and then created a life that allowed me to answer, "Of course!" to a worthwhile "Why not?" But it wasn't always easy.

In my pre-Renaissance life as a lawyer I had a busy—make that frenzied, hectic, tumultuous—practice with clients, trials, and meetings that often kept me stuck in my office like a bug on flypaper. And then there was the money. I spent the end of every calendar year agonizing about how much I had made and not made during the previous months, estimating my personal value by tallying up the dollar signs and zeroes of legal fees and partnership splits. Each December I calculated my self-worth on the balance sheet and then swore to myself, and sometimes to others, that next year would be—*it just has to be*—better. I spent over half my life chewing on the same bones: prestige, power, and money. Except I called them "professionalism," "public service," and "financial security" because those words sounded so much better. I was successful but inauthentic. Accomplished, but counterfeit. I had everything that anyone could want, but I didn't want it.

After that day in Florence, I knew that I needed to make some drastic changes to my life or it would never be the life that I wanted. But I was not at all sure that I could do it. I was fifty-eight years old, after all. My dream was to do things that people in their twenties and thirties normally do. Applying to graduate school. Going to classes. Attending seminars. Writing papers. And—scariest of all—getting grades. Holy cow! Grades? Striving for an A. Dreading a B. Most of the teachers would be younger than me. The other students would be as young as my children, and I would be an outsider. I would not fit in and I would probably fail. I nearly talked myself out of it.

Eventually though, I came to realize a very important truth. I could take the experiences of my past and repurpose them to fit the challenges of my future. After all, I had not wasted my decades. I had developed the talents that allowed me to master a demanding profession. My age did not have to be a limitation; it could be an advantage.

As this thought settled into my consciousness and became part of my mind-set, I knew—just knew—that the Personal Renaissance I wanted was lurking out there somewhere, hiding behind disappointment. I could almost see it—almost, but not quite—hiding in the tall grass of *what-can-be*, waiting for me to claim it. I had the opportunity to express my essence and live it transparently, without subterfuge. An existence without masquerade.

As I created my own Personal Renaissance, I learned that many other people were in the same psychological boat. When I told them I was going to graduate school at the age of fifty-eight because I had always wanted to earn a PhD and now I was doing it, they marveled at my determination. They praised my courage. They admired my daring. Then, almost every time, our conversation turned away from promise and opportunity and entered the dark territory of *The Three Blanks*.

"Boy, I wish I could make a few changes in my life. I am so sick of the way things are," they would often say. Then sometimes, while looking off into the middle distance, "You know, I've always wanted to be [or do] _____." They would fill in *The First Blank* with the dream they would have loved to make real. "I would be an engineer." "I would get married." "I would move to Tahiti." "I would paint landscapes." Whatever.

"Then make that happen," I would always say, encouraging them to reach for the Personal Renaissance that lurked within The First Blank. "You can. Of course you can."

"No, I can't. That simply isn't possible for me because _____." They would fill in *The Second Blank* with whatever fearful belief had stopped them in their tracks. "I'm too old," or "I'm not smart enough," or "It would be too hard," or "It would take too long," or "I can't afford it," or "I have a mortgage to pay." You get the picture.

"I used to feel the same way," I always said. "But then I discovered that there were ways to make it happen once I really wanted to. If I can do it, so can you."

"Oh, no! I'm nothing like you." The regular riposte. "You're _____." *The Third Blank* explained what it was about me, or anyone else for that matter, that made me special, peculiar, better, or more likely to succeed. The Third

Blank claimed that I was smarter or richer or younger or older or more ambitious or less ambitious. I had more to lose, or I had less to lose. Usually, none of those things were true, and even when they were (maybe I *was* older or younger), I knew that none of them really mattered. The Third Blank was not about reality; it was the dwelling place for excuses and rationalization.

The Three Blanks. Desires, fears, excuses. I listened while many of my friends let The Three Blanks keep them from the life they wanted. Maybe you're like them: making sacrifices for years—squandering your joy, your independence, maybe even the awareness of your integral self—in order to build the life that now confines you. Haven't you purchased the unsatisfactoriness of your current life with The Three Blanks? Haven't you filled in the blanks of an incomplete life with all of your refusals to live a complete one?

You may not recognize this about yourself yet, but the answer to that question is a resounding "Yes." Yes, that is indeed what you have been doing. You could have stopped filling in the blanks yesterday, or last year, or on the day you entered high school. We all could have, but we didn't.

The moral of the Personal Renaissance story is this: I am not somebody special or unique who did something that no one else can do. *I did something that anyone can do.* Something that you can do. My journey was not always easy and smooth. My luck was sometimes good and sometimes bad. I'm sure that all of us can say those very same things. In many ways I am probably a lot like you. In many ways I am like a lot of people.

I tried and I succeeded. I now live a better life than I ever lived before, and I'm here to tell you that I wouldn't go back to those pre-Renaissance days for all the big verdicts, fat retainers, and corner offices in the world.

How do we get started? Let me tell you a story.

In 1983, Paul Tsongas was the senior US senator from the state of Massachusetts. That year he learned that he had cancer and might have only a short time to live. He considered leaving the Senate to spend more time with his family and friends but there were many public issues that he was passionate about, and he knew that he would leave much work unfinished if he resigned. As he was deciding how to spend the limited future that fate had dealt him, one of his friends gave him a piece of advice that settled the matter.

"No one ever said these words on their deathbed:

'I wish I had spent more time in the office.'"

Senator Tsongas resigned from the Senate, and when his cancer went into remission, he had time to work on the issues he believed in. He could also use those extra years to enjoy and refashion his life.

Those words of advice from the senator's friend have become a cliché, but they still contain a lot of wisdom. They remind us that we should all strive to live every moment of our lives with determination.

I told that story a few months ago when I was the keynote speaker at a fund-raising event in support of a local hospice agency. Hospice workers are compassionate souls who give their time and energy to relieve the suffering and fear that often surround the nearness of death. Sometimes we think of them as selfless volunteers who give much and get little in return. But I told my audience that day that I disagreed with that image. Instead, I believe that the nearness of death can teach us that even the longest and most fabulous life is pretty short. We can learn, like Senator Tsongas did, that we must live a life that enriches us, not just one that occupies us.

"No one ever said on their deathbed, 'I wish I had spent more time in the office.'"

That's good advice, I told my audience. "But what are some *other* things that nobody wants to say on their last day?" I answered my own question with some suggestions.

No one ever says, "I'm glad I didn't take more risks."

No one ever says, "Thank goodness I never listened to my gut instincts."

No one ever says, "It's a good thing that I never followed my heart."

So before you read any further, here is a homework assignment for you: *Decide what you don't want to say with your final breath. Then, right now, start living the kind of life that won't make you have to say it.*

Think about that. Your answer to that one question will take you a long way toward defining what your Personal Renaissance will look like. Everyone will answer it differently, but one thing is certain—if you are thinking about external validation, the cheers of the crowd, fame and fortune, you are barking up the wrong tree. Leonardo da Vinci was one of humanity's greatest geniuses, but his final words revealed that he died believing himself to have been a failure. "I have offended God and mankind because my work did not reach the quality it should have." W. C. Fields was one of the biggest show-business stars of his generation, but his fame brought him no comfort. He died so unhappy that he used his final breath for a curse. "God damn the whole friggin' world and everyone in it."

But do you remember Sir Edmund Hillary? When he looked back on his life, a truly magnificent life filled with acclaim and achievement, the one thing that mattered most to him was the thing that steered him to greatness. "I have had a dream and it has come true."

What will you say? And better yet, what is the one thing that you positively do not want to have to say? Mine is this: "*I spent my days on Earth following someone else's path.*"

And so I made sure that my life would never make me have to say that. But first, I had to stop the train.

SECOND
GUIDEPOST

Do not allow yourself to live a life you will regret.

The Imaginary Train

One day your wondering about the Emergency Stop switch becomes curiosity, and the curiosity becomes fascination. A sense rises within you that you have to pull the switch, stop the train, disembark, look around, see what's outside, look ahead, and experience the externality of a world not defined by the comfortable, contained space in which you have spent your life looking at the reflection of your own changing face and the unforgiving urgency of the moments left behind.

But you sit still, just thinking about what it would be like to pull the switch. How peaceful your life would be without the constant clacketyclacketyclack *of the wheels and the roar of the engine. You imagine what it would be like if you could look around in 360 degrees and see the world for all that it is. You could walk all around, going as far as you wanted in any direction. If you saw something interesting in the distance, you could walk right up and take a closer look. If you got out of your small compartment, you might be amazed at how big the out- side world really is. How far it is to the horizon and how many things there are between here and there. Everything would stand still for you to touch it and experience its authenticity. You could see and feel and touch, and there would be no window to get in the way, no hard glass to cut you off from direct experiential contact with the unmitigated reality around you.*

CHAPTER 3

LEAVING THE PALACE

*"Time is a sort of river of passing events,
and strong is its current. No sooner is
a thing brought to sight than it is swept
by and another takes its place,
and this too will be swept away."*

MARCUS AURELIUS

When scientists want to examine an idea, they often engage in procedures called *thought experiments*: they analyze their ideas by subjecting them to tests of imagination and deep reflection. Albert Einstein solved the problem of relativity by using a thought experiment to imagine that he could ride on a beam of light. The famous story about Isaac Newton and the apple tree is not a historical fact. The falling apple was actually a thought experiment that allowed Sir Isaac to imagine and describe the workings of a gravitational universe.

The story of *The Imaginary Train* is a thought experiment, and I hope that it helps you imagine what it feels like to be carried passively through your own life. The passengers on a speeding train do not control where they are going, how long it will take to get there, or what the route will be. They just ride along and watch the world rushing past. That view outside the window, of course, is the life that you can't reach while you stay trapped in the carriage. Until you stop the train, until you exercise some positive control over the direction and velocity of your existence, you can't create your Personal Renaissance.

But before you can think about doing that, you have to convince yourself that taking control of your destiny is really the right thing to do. We are all tempted to ride along and let circumstances carry us forward without any input from us. After all, why should we make the effort to turn the world upside down? What's so great about creating a Personal Renaissance anyway?

These are tough questions and important ones. If the choice was obvious and the path was easy, then we would all have made our changes a long time ago. To understand these questions a little better, let's look at one of the world's oldest and best stories about a person who changed his life. It comes from the land of Nepal in the sixth century BC and it involves a young prince named Siddhartha.

According to legend, Siddhartha was born under miraculous circumstances. Some stories say that he was conceived in a dream. Some say that his mother was a virgin. Others claim that he sprang from her side without the pain of childbirth. His father, Suddhodana, was a great king. After Siddhartha was born, wise men told Suddhodana that his son's future was uncertain. He would either become a great king or a great religious leader. Suddhodana wanted his son to become a king, so he decreed that the prince would live a life of privilege and luxury and never be exposed to anything unpleasant or ugly. For many years that plan worked like a charm. Suddhodana built three palaces for the boy's enjoyment and filled them with every comfort and pleasure. Delicious food. Flowers and fruit trees. Beautiful art. Gorgeous women. When Siddhartha was sixteen his father arranged a marriage to a beautiful princess. They had a son, and it looked like Siddhartha would live happily ever after and become the great king that his father wanted him to be.

But one day Siddhartha's curiosity got the better of him, and he wondered what the world was like outside his palace. He ordered one of his servants, Channa by name, to hitch up a chariot and drive him around the kingdom, out in the world that he had never seen. It was an astonishing revelation for Siddhartha. He saw people going about their day-to-day business. Families with their children. Buyers and sellers in the marketplace. He was fascinated. But then he saw something that threw him for a loop. Sitting by the side of the road was a very old man. He was infirm and weak; he could hardly stand up. As the old man leaned on his crutch and struggled to his feet, Siddhartha was shocked into a confused frenzy. He had never seen such a thing. It was peculiar and strange. Was that creature even human? Everyone in Siddhartha's palace was young and attractive; they were nothing like this grotesque oddity. When Siddhartha asked Channa for an answer, the servant explained that Siddhartha was looking at an old man and that all human beings eventually get old. Even Siddhartha.

Siddhartha was shocked by that news and he didn't like it one little bit. He insisted on learning more about the outside world, so he had Channa take him on more chariot rides throughout his kingdom. Eventually he saw a sick person and then he saw a dead body. These discoveries were even more disturbing, especially when Channa explained that sickness and death were also normal and inevitable. Siddhartha could not believe what he was hearing. His life up to that moment had been ideal. Not only had he never experienced old age, disease, or death, he didn't even know that such things existed.

His worldview was that of a person whose life was made up of one perfect day after another. The universe had given him a good life, and he thought that was all there was. But now that he had looked outside of his limited, compartmentalized environment he saw that there was more to the world than the comforts of the palace. He became disquieted by what he had learned and dissatisfied with the way things had always been. One night he snuck out of the palace. He was determined to confront the suffering of genuine existence and to find a way to deal with it. He wanted to change the world, and he knew that he would first have to change himself.

He tried everything. He consulted religious traditions near and far. He spent years with monks and with hermits. He prayed and meditated for days at a time. He put himself through long fasts and hunger strikes. Nothing worked. None of those things gave him any insights about how a normal person could live a happy life in a world filled with suffering. Finally, when he had almost starved himself to death with fasting, a young girl showed pity and offered him food. When Siddhartha accepted that simple act of human kindness, it made him realize that self-denial did not hold the answers he was seeking. In order to cope with suffering, human beings have to recognize that it exists. We have to face it in order to face it down. If we are going to survive in the world, we have to become part of the world. We have to deal with some awful things in the real world, that is true; but we also have to learn how to accept the kindness and love that the world has to offer. That was Siddhartha's discovery.

Some readers may recognize this story. Siddhartha sat under a tree and meditated nonstop for days and days on his new insight, and he eventually achieved a level of understanding that transformed him into the Buddha: the Awakened One. He spent the next forty-five years of his life teaching people how to immerse themselves in the authenticity of the world and still live happy and satisfying lives. The Buddha's lessons teach us that we don't have to live in the kind of palaces that Suddhodana built for Siddhartha in order to be happy, and his teachings have become the foundation of one of the world's great religions. Today, it is estimated that the Buddha's lessons about living are followed by about 500 million people around the world, and that number grows every year. Many people rely on the Buddha's teachings to help them navigate the difficulties of the world with wisdom and peace of mind.

But here's a thought: what if Siddhartha had never left the palace? What if he never became enlightened? No one forced Siddhartha to leave his palace. He didn't have any obligation to go out there and save the world. He was doing fine just the way he was, and just because people were getting old and sick and dying, that didn't mean that it was up to him to fix anything. He could have stayed put, and sooner or later he would have learned as much about the bad things in life as anybody needs to know. He would have gotten older, he was bound to get sick, and sooner or later everyone dies. Why bother traipsing around Nepal, starving and meditating and sitting under trees, trying to decode the universe? He didn't owe anybody a thing. He could have stayed right where he was. Maybe he would have ended up the happiest man on earth. Who knows?

Some Buddhist scholars say that Siddhartha was preordained to become the Awakened One. Maybe he was destined from birth, or even before that, to achieve enlightenment and spread that teaching throughout the world. Maybe. But one thing is certain about that story: enlightenment did not just fall onto his lap while he luxuriated at home eating pistachios with his concubines. He didn't wake up to the meaning of his life by sitting still in his palace—or by riding on a comfortable train. He had to go out there and chase it down. He had to leave his old life behind. He already had everything that a man could desire, but he had to give it up if he was ever going to find something better.

That was the dilemma that faced Siddhartha. It's the same dilemma that faces all of us. Will we tolerate a life of incompleteness, or will we accept, even invite, an element of struggle? Do we sit tight with a bird in the hand, or do we dare to face the thousand swarming bees waiting for us out there in the bush? The doubts and trepidation you may feel are your past talking to you. Your past is telling you that life is good just the way it is, and if you rock the boat you might fall out and get soaked by the rough and risky waters of uncertainty.

Maybe Siddhartha would have been better off if he had just stayed in the palace. Maybe the world would have been a better place if he had never found that meditation tree at all. Who can say? The problem with the future is that you can't really understand it until it's the past. Every decision is perilous. All of life is risk. But since living is mandatory, you might as well choose to do it for real. Maybe, just maybe, that safe, secure train carriage is the most dangerous place of all.

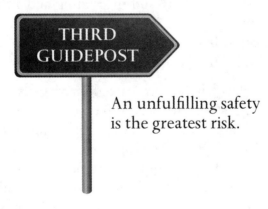

THIRD GUIDEPOST

An unfulfilling safety is the greatest risk.

The Imaginary Train

Sometimes you have seen other people walking in the lands beyond your window. You have looked at them through the transparency of your reflected face and marveled at their exposure to the world. They had no safe carriage to shield them from rain, cold, or reality. They could walk and run or stop and sit. They are not tethered to a track or to a rail; they risk getting lost as they wander far and wide. Their rambling freedom exposes them to the cold and to hazards that you will never know, not as long as you stay in your carriage. But the same wanderlust that condemns them to peril and uncertainty allows them to enter into any future they create for themselves. Unlike you, they are not just moving points on a one-dimensional vector that leads from wherever they started on a path they don't control to a destination they can't select. With every step, each trainless wanderer becomes a pioneer on a risky, glad adventure.

While you think of those souls of daring and endangerment, your train enters a long, dark tunnel. With only blackness beyond the window your face is mirrored crisp and sharp.

In that dark clarity you look older than you imagined. Smaller. Less complete. You look again at Emergency Stop, and you contemplate frontiers.

CHAPTER 4

The Alumni Bulletin

"There are only two mistakes
one can make along the road to truth;
not going all the way, and not starting."
Buddha

As long ago as my senior year in college I wanted to go
to graduate school, earn a humanities doctorate, and teach.
I had studied literature and classics as an undergraduate and
I loved them. I read Homer and Plato, Milton and Byron, I
wrote papers about them and even won a prize. But when it
came time to look at graduate schools, my professors counseled me about the awful state of the academic job market.
They described grim prospects for finding employment and
urged me to forget academia and look for a different career. I
found it confusing that men who led such privileged and pleasant lives teaching at wonderful schools, reading and studying
great literature, enjoying the company of intelligent colleagues
and students, were so negative about their work. Nonetheless,
they were my teachers, they definitely had my best interests
at heart, and I felt that they knew best. So I abandoned the

whole graduate-school-and-faculty career path and looked for something else.

Some of my friends were history and political science majors who were gearing up to take the law school admission test. I had never thought about becoming a lawyer but the test only took one day, I could take it on my campus, and I didn't have any better prospects, so I figured, "Why not?" I took the test, and to my great surprise I absolutely aced it. When my academic adviser found out, he introduced me to the college's prelaw advisor. Pretty soon I was filling out law school applications, lining up letters of reference, applying for scholarships, and getting accepted. Events were taking command, and for the first time I had that feeling that my life was being propelled forward in directions I couldn't control. I could almost hear the *clackety-clack-clack* of the steel wheels on railroad tracks. I had started riding *The Imaginary Train*.

Law school roared past me. I discovered that the admission test score was no fluke; I really did have a gift for the specialized kind of thinking and logic that the law requires. All around me, other law students studied twenty hours a day, starved themselves, and became hermits. A few had nervous breakdowns. They nearly killed themselves for grades and the status of a law degree. I, on the other hand, sailed through those years making high grades and earning one award after another. When one of my roommates told me that it wasn't fair that he worked day and night for mediocre grades while I cruised my way to the top of the class, I had to agree with him. It wasn't fair at all. But that's exactly how it happened, and I graduated with honors. Now what?

The truth of the matter was that while learning the law came easy for me, I had no idea what lawyers did for a living. When I was growing up my family had been dirt poor, and we didn't exactly rub elbows with the professional classes. I never knew a lawyer until my older brother married one, but they lived far away and I didn't know very much about her work. I learned most of what I knew about the practice of law by watching lawyer shows on television. TV lawyers were always defending innocent people who were falsely accused of murder, so that's what I thought I would be doing, too. After passing the bar exam, I started sharing office space with an older local attorney and I waited for the innocent murder cases to start rolling in.

And I waited. And then I waited some more. I spent my first few weeks as a lawyer sharpening pencils, reading the newspaper, and wondering where my plan had gone wrong. Weren't there enough murder cases to go around? Were my classmates getting them all? No, that couldn't be it, because they were all doing boring stuff that I had never even heard of. Searching titles, taking depositions (*What in the world was a deposition?* I wondered), and suing and defending lawsuits. Lawsuits! People suing each other for money! Could that really be true? Were there really lawyers who did that for a living? I was totally clueless and getting more and more frustrated every day.

Well, eventually I got a call to help an established lawyer handle a murder trial. Then I got another case, and then the local judges started appointing me to represent people who couldn't afford to pay for private lawyers. My cases got more interesting and more important, and before I knew it I was named in the first edition of a national directory called *The Best Lawyers in America*. All at once I was a rising star in the profession.

Clackety-clackety-clack-clack.

I won't bore you with a day-by-day account of the next three decades, but they were pretty wild. Two unhappy marriages.

Two bitter divorces. Two spectacular and wonderful children. A law partnership formed and dissolved. Another law firm. More cases. More money. Faster cars. A bigger house.

And then . . .

A copy of my college's alumni magazine appeared in my mailbox. There was a story about my classmate Fred who had just been promoted to full professor at a major university. Fred had been an English major like me and had even been in some of my classes. After I graduated and went on to law school I had forgotten all about Fred. Until the day that magazine arrived.

After college, Fred went on to inhabit the experience that he wanted all along. When professors and experts told him that the academic job market stunk and that he would be crazy to pursue his dream Fred went ahead and pursued it anyway. And he caught it. There was a picture of him in the magazine. He was sitting at a round table with a class of interested students. He was wearing a pair of shorts and a denim shirt, and he had a thick book of poetry open in front of him. He was gesturing with his hands, and the students were listening intently.

I don't know if Fred had ever heard his life *clackety-clack-ing* away from him, but he sure looked happy now. Existentially happy. As happy as I would have been if I had been Fred.

At about the same time that I read Fred's story, the prelaw advisor from my college days announced that he was finally retiring. His field of expertise, constitutional law and civil rights, was a subject that I had mastered in one courtroom after another and I was positive—*positive*—that no one could teach those subjects to college students better than I could. When the college advertised for his replacement, I jumped at the opening. I wrote a beautiful letter of application about my deep love for the college and the dedication I would give its students—and then they hired a young guy right out of graduate school. I got a two-line letter saying that they wished it was different but they really wanted someone with a PhD and all I had was a law degree. When I read that letter I was disappointed and a little angry. I didn't really believe that a diploma, even an important one, would make anyone a better teacher. I wasted a little time grousing about the academic snobbery that led some people to believe that only doctors of philosophy belonged on college faculties. But then I realized that since colleges preferred to hire PhDs I had three choices.

1. I could say "forget it" and keep riding the law train.

2. I could complain and gripe and moan about it while I failed to be hired over and over again.

3. I could just get the damn degree.

I received my doctorate about forty years later than I expected, but I will tell you from the bottom of my heart that it was not too late. Maya Angelou was right when she said, "As long as you're breathing, it's never too late to do some good." I believe that rule also applies to doing some good for yourself.

I know that the idea of being a PhD college professor may not appeal to you in the slightest. I'll be the first to admit that it is not for everyone. Here's what you have to figure out: what is *your* Personal Renaissance? What is the life that awaits you? Where should you go when you get off your train?

That question has occupied and frustrated many of the most powerful thinkers since the dawn of time. We can find it reflected in the work of great poets and scholars from throughout the ages and in the commonplace, everyday musings of men and women everywhere. Have you ever listened to a graduation speaker say that the day was called "commencement" because it was the beginning of a new experience? Have you ever seen an inspirational calendar with the January promise that "Today Is the First Day of the Rest of Your Life"? Have you ever sat around late at night with a few friends and some empty wine bottles pondering the meaning of life? If so, you don't need Einstein or Plato to tell you that the search for life's fulfillment is complicated. One good place to start looking is in the work of a nineteenth-century German philosopher.

Friedrich Nietzsche was a thirty-year-old professor at the University of Basel in 1874 when he wrote a short book of meditations. He was wrestling with the same questions that we ask over a hundred years later. How can we determine our life's purpose? After we have said no to all the stuff that doesn't work for us, what should we then say yes to? What comes next? For Nietzsche, the best answer to "How shall I live?" was to let your spirit, your consciousness, become an explorer that examines the world and itself until it finds the thing that has guided it and nurtured it and brought it to the moment of discovery. Nietzsche's advice was hard and simple: we must look deep inside ourselves and find the thing—the one thing—that we have always wanted most, the unrealized desire that has elevated us, the unreified dream that has refused to take no for an answer. The quest for the purpose of your life takes place in the world all around you, but the question that you must answer comes from deep within yourself.

That question, simple but all-consuming, is this: What is the thing you love the most?

I believe that we all know what we love about life and that we can all identify the thing that we want the most, or the thing we want more of. We all know, if we stop and think honestly about ourselves, what it takes to fill in The First Blank. "I have always wanted to _____." We have to search with honest deliberation and be willing to accept the discoveries we make along the way. It may take some work, but I will suggest to you that avoiding that search is much worse. If you want to find your own New World, first you must conquer your Life's Frontier.

I am writing this chapter after watching my dear friend Sarah take the oath of office as a judge of the Court of Common Pleas of Dauphin County, Pennsylvania. The ceremony was held in Courtroom One of the Dauphin County Courthouse. Courtroom One takes up almost half of the fifth floor of the courthouse. It is the county's largest courtroom. Portraits of old judges line the walls, and long wooden pews fill its public section. It felt a little strange to be back there after being away from the practice of law for so long. I defended dozens of criminal cases in Courtroom One, many murders, many acquittals, and some convictions. The energy from my life as a lawyer was strong in that room, and it electrified me as I watched her take the oath of office. I could feel my very first not-guilty verdict from when I was a young lawyer of twenty-five. I could feel the time one of my clients was sentenced to death in that room, and I could feel the several whom I saved from that fate.

Courtrooms can resonate like haunted spaces; there is so much emotional and psychic energy stored up within their four walls. I was happy to support Sarah on her big day, but I was not happy to be back in that room.

Sarah has all of the tools that a judge should have. She is smart and honest and kind and she is devoted to justice. She will work hard and she will have compassion for the less privileged and not-so-lucky people who appear before her. Courtrooms are scary. Most people do not end up there on purpose. Instead, they usually kick and scream in anguish as they are dragged through the back door by bad luck, mistakes, or moral catastrophes. Sarah will know that and she will do as much as she can to restore some fairness to the customary chaos of the court system. More than that, she will insist that others also act fairly and decently. And so she will be a wonderful judge.

Not only will she do a good job, but this is the job that she has wanted for a long time. Many years passed her by while she was longing to be a judge. She was always a good lawyer, but that was not where her personal authenticity dwelled and she knew it. Being a lawyer was not, and never would be, the Nietzschean thing that Sarah loved. Today, as she raised her hand and swore to discharge her new duties with fidelity to the law and the Constitution, she was rebirthed into her Personal Renaissance. I was thrilled to watch it happen.

Would you like to be a judge? Many people would. You make decisions that affect people's lives. You enjoy the respect of your community. You can contribute to society and make a real difference. It's an important job and a powerful one. And let's not forget that everyone is required by law to call you "Your Honor" and stand up whenever you walk into a room. Sweet.

But do you know what else I felt while I watched Sarah's ceremony? Relief. I was relieved that it was her and not me taking that oath and putting on that robe and ascending to the judge's bench. Why? Because I would *hate* that job. I don't want to have to judge anybody. First of all, I don't have the stomach to throw people in jail even if they deserve it. But more importantly, judges have to ignore their own views of right and wrong because they are obliged to decide every case according to a boatload of legal technicalities. They swear that they will ignore their own personal preferences.

"Fidelity to the law" means you don't always get to do whatever you yourself believe is fair. Personally, I would find that terribly frustrating. When I was a lawyer, the things that I *did* like about it were that I could pick the battles I wanted to fight and I could pick the side I wanted to fight for. So being a judge would not be for me.

When I found out that Sarah was going to be a judge, I called to congratulate her. "I know you think I'm crazy," she laughed when she answered the phone.

"Not at all," I assured her, and I meant it. She had a thing she loved and it was not going to be reified until she got off the being-a-lawyer train and started walking in the direction of her Personal Renaissance. She had to pull Emergency Stop on her inauthentic lawyer life, and that's what she did. I told her that her dream was not my dream, but that she deserved to have her own personal, private, deep-in-her-heart-of-hearts dream come true. After all, that was the only one that was supposed to come true for her. I may not want to live her Renaissance life, but I don't have to. So I could be thrilled for her without an ounce of reserve.

Was Siddhartha right to leave the palace? Should you get off the train? Of course. Siddhartha's refusal to stay content with inadequacy has allowed billions of people to strive for improvement over the course of thousands of years. All of those strivers have been helped to escape their individual Dark Ages and create the Personal Renaissance of their own essence. Some of them have even succeeded.

Professor? Artist? Doctor? Chef? Lawyer? Writer? Parent? Judge? Inventor? Merchant? Athlete? Star? Whatever. What will the true authenticity of your real life look like? How do you *reify* the thing you love? In other words, how do you turn it from a dream into a thing? How can you make it real?

When you find and pursue the thing you love, it might not make you another Siddhartha. You may not improve a billion lives. But you will definitely and positively improve at least one: yours.

FOURTH GUIDEPOST

The thing you love the most is on the wild side of Life's Frontier.

The Imaginary Train

As the train carries you onward through the darkness, you stand up and walk to the switch. It feels unexpectedly comfortable, it fits your hand. You look at the window and watch the blackness rumble past. The train leaves the tunnel and the world outside the carriage is once again bright and blurry. But then, all of an instant, you see clouds of steam erupt from the piston brakes and the wheels. An insistent scream—SCREECH!—rises against the steel rails beneath them. You lurch forward and then catch yourself as you become aware of what has happened. You inhale deeply, one breath full of terror and possibility as you realize that you have finally pulled the switch.

PART TWO

Frontier

*"From the conditions of frontier life came
intellectual traits of profound importance….
The result is that to the frontier the American
intellect owes its striking characteristics."*

FREDERICK JACKSON TURNER

INTRODUCTION

Before Turner's speech at the Chicago Exposition, most historians took it for granted that the American character, if there really was such a thing, came from Europe. The Pilgrims, the Puritans, and all of the other pioneers who traveled to the Western Hemisphere brought their cultures and national identities with them. Those identities and cultures took root on New World soil and eventually spawned a fresh national identity. This was the so-called *Teutonic Germ Theory* and it said that Americanism was something different from Europeanism, but it wasn't different by very much. If you wanted to see where America started, the experts said, look to the past— across the deep, vast ocean to the east.

Turner had a mind-bendingly different idea. He was a student of geology as well as history and he understood evolution. His interest in natural environments gave him a keen sense of space and time, and it allowed him to see that the American identity was not a clone of the European identity. Instead, it evolved out of something unprecedented and new. He believed that it was not the past that created America; it was the promise of an undiscovered future. If you wanted to find America, said Turner, don't look to the east across the ocean. Look to the west across the mountains. Look into the unsettled land of wild uncertainty and unmitigated risk. Look beyond the frontier.

The frontier was a bold idea. It postulated a vibrant boundary between the settled land to the east and the unexplored and (presumably) wild land to the west. On one side of the frontier line was safety, comfort, and refuge. On the other side was—who knows? An ancient mapmaker had once warned sailors away from unknown seas by marking his maps with the claim, "Hic Sunt Dracones." *There are dragons here.* The unexplored lands of the American West were scarcely less scary than that. Nonetheless, seeking fortune, people established new communities, and by taming the wild land under their feet they expanded the envelope of civilization. They poured across the frontier line, and by crossing it they defined it. The wilderness was always one short step ahead of their westward progress. The boundary of the known world moved along with them, traveling in their wagons and their shoes. That was what Turner realized—America had a moving frontier. As Turner himself explained it, "In this advance, the frontier is the outer edge of the wave—the meeting point between savagery and civilization."

The wilderness of the West was ripe for the taking. All you needed was a hero's courage and a gambler's heart. The descendants of explorers who had sailed across hostile seas now set out across a continent of unknown perils and uncertain opportunities. Their ingenuity and verve created a people with burning desires to be independent and free. It was not America's yesterdays that created her, said Turner, it was her covert tomorrows. The frontier traveled alongside the pioneers and taught them to be democratic and free. The draw of the frontier was the Renaissance of individualism.

Heading into lands where there might, after all, be dragons, the seekers and the strivers created new lives and new identities. They moved the line between comfortable mediocrity and the birth of a new potential a little bit at a time, mile by mile, sometimes inch by inch. The reification of their dream took resolve, planning, faith, and action. It could not be conjured or contrived.

CHAPTER 5

MAKING LIFE

"The meaning of life is to find your gift.
The purpose of life is to give it away."
PABLO PICASSO

It was 1932, and Celestia Robertson was worried about her
sister's arthritis.

Celestia's sister Anna Mary was seventy-two years old and
she had lived a hard life. They had been born into a poor family
in upstate New York, and Anna Mary worked on the family
farm from her early childhood. There was a one-room school-
house nearby, but she couldn't go there much. There was no
money for warm clothing, so when the weather got cold she
had to stay home. When she was twelve, she was sent to work
as a "hired girl" in the home of a wealthy family. For fifteen
years she did their cleaning, housework, and chores and never
really had much of a life of her own. Finally, when she was
twentyseven, she met and married a farmer named Thomas. It
was 1887.

Anna Mary gave birth to ten children. Five died in infancy.
The family planned to move to South Carolina for better

prospects but they only made it as far as Virginia. They ended up renting land there and working as tenant farmers. Anna Mary worked to supplement the farm income by churning butter and making potato chips. She grew to love Virginia, but Thomas wanted to move back to New York so away they went. They settled outside a little town called Eagle Bridge, and Thomas died there twenty-two years later. Anna Mary was alone now, so she went to live with her daughter in nearby Hoosic Falls. She was sixty-seven.

Throughout her many hardships, one thing that had always given her pleasure was embroidering pictures of rural life. She called them her "worsted pictures," and she gave them away for free to anyone who wanted them. But Anna Mary was getting older now, and her sister Celestia was worried because the arthritis made it hard for her to hold a needle. It looked like Anna Mary would have to stop making pictures.

But Celestia remembered that when the sisters were young, Anna Mary liked to paint. The family that couldn't afford school clothes surely could not afford art supplies, so Anna Mary made her own paint out of fruit juice. Paintbrushes were thicker than embroidery needles, reasoned Celestia, and they might be easier for an arthritic hand to hold. So Celestia suggested that Anna Mary switch to a new medium. It was a Personal Renaissance idea that grew out of unhappiness and expressed the thing she loved—creativity—and it worked like a charm.

Before too long, Anna Mary was painting her rural farm scenes instead of embroidering them. She painted on paper and cardboard, and eventually gave some pictures to the local druggist, who agreed to sell them in his store. The small ones were three dollars and the bigger ones were five. Every once in a while she would sell one, and it made her happy.

One day in 1938 when Anna Mary was seventy-eight years old, an art dealer named Louis Caldor was driving through Hoosic Falls on vacation. He stopped by the drugstore and saw Anna Mary's paintings. He bought them all, found the artist at her daughter's house, and bought some more. It may have been the greatest bargain in the history of modern art. Within a year, three of her paintings were in a show at New York City's Museum of Modern Art, and a year after that she had her own show at the prestigious Gallerie St. Etienne. By 1940, eighty-year-old Anna Mary was world-famous, and the paintings that she called her "old-timey" pictures were recognized as masterpieces of American primitive modernity. Art collectors and galleries were buying them for tens of thousands of dollars. One of her paintings later sold at auction for over a million. Not many people called her Anna Mary anymore. By then, everyone in the world knew her as Grandma Moses.

By the time Grandma Moses died in 1961 at the age of ninety-one she was one of America's most beloved public figures. She had dined in the White House. President Truman played his piano for her. *Mademoiselle* magazine honored her as a Young Woman of the Year in 1948 when she was eighty-eight years young. The National Press Club called her one of the five most newsworthy women in 1950 when she was ninety-one. Russell Sage College gave her an honorary doctorate, and the Moore College of Art and Design gave her another one. Her autobiography became a best seller. A documentary film about her life was nominated for an Academy Award. Her artwork hung in museums around the world, and she was acclaimed as one of the greatest artists of the age. How did she react to such spectacular popularity and success? Just like this: "I look back on my life like a good day's work," she said. "Life is what we make it, always has been, always will be."

What made Grandma Moses a great painter? She wasn't great when she was a child artist, that's for sure. Nor when she was a hired girl, a farm wife, a butter churner, or an embroiderer. She was never a great painter until adversity forced her arthritic hand. Her greatness arose out of a dissatisfaction with her circumstances and a deeply felt need for the thing she loved the most. For Anna Mary that thing was creativity. She thrived on artistic creation. It nourished her, it fulfilled her. As long as she could hold the embroidery needle, she could not be a great painter. The arthritis that took away Anna Mary's needlepoint gave the world Grandma Moses. When Celestia put a brush in her hand, that was Anna Mary's Personal Renaissance.

Many people today have heard of Grandma Moses, but not everyone knows that her genius sprouted from her unwillingness to accept a crippling affliction. We don't know what the world of modern art would have been like if she had never developed arthritis, but we do know that she painted as a child and then gave it up. She didn't start again until her unfulfilled creative spirit felt an urgency to be rebirthed as something new. Without that urgency, she would almost certainly have kept on riding the arthritic-farm-widow train and lived out her years with her daughter in a comfortable, but obscure, old age. She might have accepted that she was fated to live a life without creativity. But she didn't.

It is worth remembering Grandma Moses's lesson that Renaissance begins with dissatisfaction and culminates with individual fulfillment. "Life is what we make it, always has been, always will be." Yes indeed.

The speeding train of our lives will carry us forward through the days of joy and sorrow until sooner or later we have simply had enough of an existence that tolerates incompleteness. The exact moment that any particular person stops his or her train is unpredictable. Some people never act and they spend their whole lives riding through a landscape that they have never chosen. But for you and me, we will act. Some will do it sooner, others later. Both are okay. It's never too soon, and—here is something else worth remembering—it's never too late. It is always possible to decide that *now* is the right time. Every day that we wake up alive and breathing gives us another opportunity to stop our rushing train whenever the moment is right for us. There is no statute of limitations for Renaissance.

Often when I speak at public gatherings about creating a Personal Renaissance, I see eyes around the audience getting wider and sometimes moister. It seems that the greatest emotional reaction comes from my story about *The Imaginary Train* and the Emergency Stop. When I mingle with the crowd, many people want to tell me why my story has resonated so deeply with them.

"Can I tell you about the time I got off that train?" some will ask. Naturally, I say "Of course."

One woman told me that she and her husband decided one day to sell their house and most of their belongings, buy a motor home, and travel all around the country. They both gave up good jobs. Their children and grandchildren lived near their old home. They had tons of friends, a nice neighborhood, and a comfortable life, but they knew that their real life lay somewhere outside of that existence. "It was a big step," she explained with a smile, "and many of our friends thought that we were crazy. But we have never regretted our decision. It was just something we knew we needed to do. Our old life was not satisfying us, and we had to do something really drastic. We felt that we needed to make a change. Do you understand what I mean?" she asked. Yes, I did.

No two people experience that need the same way, but I heard a wonderful story from a direct-sales cosmetics rep who came to one of my talks. She had been married and then divorced, and she raised two daughters to become young ladies who would make any parent proud. She had what she thought of as "a great life" but she had always felt a nagging dissatisfaction that made her wonder. "I used to wake up and look around my lovely home and say to myself, *What am I doing here?*" She told me that she had gotten off of her personal *Imaginary Train* after her youngest daughter graduated from high school. Until then she felt as if she was bound to the regular paycheck and the stable, predictable life that her steady job provided. "But when I had that empty nest," she explained with a twinkle in her eye, "I was free to strike out on my own."

I have heard variations of that story over and over again. "I couldn't do it before. I had to wait until _____" — whatever and whenever. I don't know much about the life of that cosmetic sales rep or anything about her own particular circumstances, but I do believe that we can all stop our trains whenever we decide. Sometimes that is a wise decision. Sometimes it is not. Jobs, mortgages, tuition payments, and more can all impose real obligations upon us that we would be irresponsible to ignore. I know that in my particular case I didn't pull the switch until my children no longer needed my financial support. Remember, my afternoon at the Piper's Thumb came after my daughter's college graduation and my son's completion of graduate school. Until then, I was the one with responsibilities and people counting on me in ways that I could not ethically avoid. So I waited for my opportunity.

Certainly, I could have stopped my train before I did if I was willing to accept much harder and greater sacrifices. I could have sold my house to pay my daughter's college tuition. I could have lived in a tent while I waited for the graduate school to decide on my application, and after that I could have lived in a student dorm with the eighteen-year-olds. But I wasn't going to do any of those things. I knew that I would be turning my comfortable lifestyle upside down and I was ready to do that, but I wasn't going to be stupid about it. Renaissance does not require you to dash off some foolhardy cliff of impetuosity and fall to your doom on the rocks of sacrifice below. Closing my law practice and starting school much sooner than I did would have been unrealistic. I waited until I believed that I could fulfill my responsibility to myself—the responsibility to live the kind of authentic life that would express the things I loved—without violating my very real responsibilities to others. I waited until I didn't think I had to wait any longer, and then I embraced the uncertainty and struck the frontier.

Sometimes we can fall into the trap of pretending that we are being cautiously responsible when all we are really doing is procrastinating. If we are not careful, we can mistake the discouraging inner voice of "it will never work" for the reasonable advice of prudence. It's a fine line between responsibility and rationalization, but the line is very real. We get off the train when we can. And even then, we usually do not get off until we know for sure that we must. Do I regret not making harder and greater sacrifices and stopping my train sooner? Sometimes. But I don't beat myself up about it. Getting off the roaring train that rushes you past an unlived life is rewarding. It is enriching, satisfying, fulfilling, and integrating—but it does take effort.

As long as you can still embroider, you probably aren't ready to start painting.

Whenever I am tempted to wonder if I waited too long, I remember that if I had pulled Emergency Stop the year or even the day before I did, my train would have stopped at a different place. An earlier place. Somewhere past and passed. The days when I did nothing but ride the train were not wasted; they brought me to the moment of my personal truth. They gave me the time I needed to become willing and brave. I believe that we will all be delivered to the exact right place. Every instant of our lives has contributed to making us who we are right now.

My own particular destination has been perfect. And so it will be for you. You will define for yourself the right time to pull the switch on your incomplete life. When you do, you are likely to discover that your train has brought you to the ideal place for you to put aside the linearity that you never chose. You will recognize it as a spot for valorizing personal authenticity. You will take another step and then another, settling into the sunshine and the breeze, absorbing all around you as you and the world get to know one another.

Your why and your when will coincide. Remember Grandma Moses: "Life is what we make it." Whenever.

FIFTH GUIDEPOST

There is no statute of limitations on Renaissance. You always set out to cross your Life's Frontier from wherever you are right now.

The Imaginary Train

You didn't think that it would be so loud. The steel wheels SCREECH against the steel track as the train goes from sixty miles per hour to zero. The force of inertia throws you forward, and you have to grab onto a seat-back or else you would tumble helplessly. For the first few seconds you need the support of the nearest seat to keep from toppling over out of control and topsy-turvy. You hold on tight as the rushing panorama outside the windows moves slower and slower and slower.

The first thought that passes through your mind is "Are you nuts? Are you insane? Why did you do something as crazy as that? No one forced you to pull that switch. Did you do it out of curiosity? For a thrill? Just for fun? To see what would happen?" Now you have to figure out what to do if the train really does come to a stop. Maybe you should just sit back down and wait for it to start rolling again. After all, you have no idea what might happen if you were to get out of this cozy, comfortable carriage and enter the strange and unfamiliar world outside. It certainly won't be as safe and secure as the life you already have on the train. You might get lost. You could trip over something, a rock or a fallen branch or a hole in the ground. You could get hurt. There could be rain. It might be cold. You might get sick. One thing seems certain to you: the outside world is unlike anything you have ever experienced, and if you do get off the train you are going to have to figure out how to deal with that world. If you decide to go out there in the midst of all of the uncertainty and strangeness, you will need a plan. You will have to learn new things as you go along. It won't be easy. It may be harder than you can even imagine. There is literally no way for you to anticipate what your life would be like if you get off the train. No one can predict the future, after all. You would have to be resilient, ready to face adversity, and prepared for disappointments and hardships. You would need courage.

Why bother? No one is here to shove you out that door. No one is pushing you off the train. You can just wait for it to start going again and then ignore that silly Emergency Stop switch forever. Sit back down in your seat. Relax. Listen to the soothing and familiar clackety-clackety-clack. Watch the world keep roaring past you. The train may be boring and isolating and confining. It may restrict you and limit your options and prevent you from experiencing a total life. So what if it narrows your horizons, shrinks your potential, disconnects you from completeness? What's so bad about that? At least it's safe. And after all, haven't things been pretty good for you up until now?

You know that pretty soon all forward motion will stop. Why did you do this? Why did you do it now? How can you possibly know the right thing to do next?

CHAPTER 6

The Immediacy of Resolve

"This is the right time,
and this is the right thing."
Sir Thomas More

George Milton and Lennie Small were a couple of down-on-their-luck farm workers during the Great Depression. They traveled around California taking whatever jobs they could find and accepting whatever pay they could get. Like many people who are thrown together by fate and chance, they were an odd pair of friends. George was small and quick, smart and capable. Lennie, by contrast, was mentally disabled and had a hard time adjusting to new surroundings and new people. Lennie's disability made him intellectually slow, "dim-witted" in the parlance of the times, but physically he was a giant. Huge and hulking, he could easily outwork most other farmhands, but the combination of his outsized physical strength and his mental slowness led him into awkward and dangerous situations. George had to take care of him and shepherd him through whatever new circumstances they encountered. Without George to protect him, Lennie, in spite of his great strength, would not survive.

Together, George and Lennie were poor, uneducated, homeless, maladjusted, and desperate. They had no money, no advantages, and no prospects. But there is one thing that they did have—they had a goal. Not a vague and shapeless goal, their goal was clear and well defined. It was specific, detailed, appealing, and attainable. They were going to keep working, save their money, pool their resources, and buy a small farm. They would grow some crops, live off the fat of the land, and Lennie would raise rabbits. It seemed like a good idea.

They were two guys who were industrious but incomplete. Decent but imperfect. They worked hard their whole lives, faced many difficulties, and surmounted many obstacles, and they mitigated their bad circumstances by setting a goal to improve their future. They held on to a bellyful of optimism, and they expected their best days to lie ahead.

I don't think George and Lennie spent much time reading books about becoming successful or attracting their own destiny, but even if they had studied the whole popular self-help library they couldn't have done a much better job of following the standard canon of personal achievement. They identified a worthy goal. They made it detailed and specific. They invested it with their desire. That's what a thousand books and programs teach, and if those things were enough, then pretty soon we could have expected George to be a successful farmer and Lennie to be a happy rabbit rancher.

But there was an unpleasant truth waiting for Lennie and George and for everyone else who seeks comfort in the practice of goal-setting. *The fallow and barren corners of our lives will not blossom and bear fruit just because we carry a goal around in our pocket, or even in our heart.*

Really? Why won't they? If we know what we want, write it down, read it every day, tape it to our mirror, and believe-to-achieve, then why won't that work? Hasn't that been the teaching of generations of self-help gurus, shamans, senseis, teachers, and life coaches? Yes indeed, it has been exactly that, and I suppose that if we had magic powers, a fairy godmother, or the genie of the lamp, then we could all be gladly transformed by the power of raw desire. However, once we rule out the possibility of magical intervention, we should cast aside the temptation to believe that goals, all by themselves, have some special power to change our lives.

Because here's the thing:

They don't.

By now, you may have recognized George and Lennie as the main characters of John Steinbeck's classic American novel *Of Mice and Men*. Published in 1937 at the height of the Great Depression, the book recounts the goals of two common men and (spoiler alert) describes the terrible events that frustrate their happiness and lead to Lennie's death at George's hand. Throughout the book George hopes that the fruit of his goal-setting will allow him to become self-sufficient, to become the "somebody" that he aspires to be. But Steinbeck's story tells us that anybody who places all of his or her hopes in goal-setting assumes the risk of becoming a miserable nobody whose unfulfilled and doubtful future lurks just one bad break beyond their reach.

In fact, the book's title comes from an old poetic warning about goal-setting. In 1785 the Scottish poet Robert Burns warned his readers, "The best-laid schemes o' mice an' men gang aft agley"—in other words, the goals we set get all messed up, they go astray, they turn out badly.

That is certainly what happened to George and Lennie. But Burns has an even more dire warning. Failed goals are not just frustrating; they are positively dangerous to our well-being and to our happiness. Here is a stanza from Burns's poem "To a Mouse" (I'm going to convert the original Scottish dialect to make it easier to understand).

The best laid schemes of mice and men

Often go astray,

And leave us nothing but grief and pain,

For promised joy! . . .

And forward, though I cannot see,

I guess and fear!

When our goals don't come true, Burns warns, that failure consumes us with "grief and pain," it ruins our optimism, and it makes us dread our future with a fearful anticipation. There is nothing left for us to do but "guess and fear" about what may come next.

What's going on here? Was Steinbeck crazy? Was Burns? If goal-setting is as valuable and powerful as all of its proponents would have us believe, then why do these two literary geniuses tell us such a different story? Where is the truth in all of this?

Any criticism of the presumed power of goal-setting is bound to be a little controversial. It seems that the whole wide world loves goals and goal-setting. Indeed, in the year 2000 the organization that represents the whole wide world—the United Nations, with its 193 member countries—goal-set an eight-pronged plan for the future. These Millennial Development Goals would eradicate extreme hunger and poverty, ensure environmental sustainability, and do six other wonderful things for all mankind. Even better, because goals have such awesome power they would have all of those problems solved by 2015.

Oops.

I recently did an Internet search for "goal setting." I got over 12 million hits. A search for books about goals brought up 24,000 titles. That number may be somewhat inflated. I think some of those books are about hockey or soccer, but you get the point. Even the Bible tells us that St. Paul set spiritual goals for himself. Who am I to say that goal-setting isn't enough?

It always helps to define our terms, so let's start there. What is a goal anyway? The *Oxford English Dictionary* defines *goal* as "the object to which effort or ambition is directed" and "an end or result towards which behavior is consciously or unconsciously directed." Other dictionary definitions include "the object of a person's ambition" and "something you are trying to do or achieve." Aristotle thought that mankind had only one true goal, a perfect state of being that he called *eudemonia*, and that all other achievements like health, wealth, love, success, and family were just intermediate accomplishments along the way. Sigmund Freud thought that the ultimate goal of life was stillness and peace. In *Julius Caesar*, Shakespeare has Brutus describe goals as "ventures" that men and women must pursue throughout "the voyage of their life" if they don't want to be "bound in shallows and in miseries."

There are many other definitions and concepts of goals, and although the words and descriptions differ, they all have one important thing in common:

Goal achievement is always something that can exist only in the future. It can never change your life right now.

Not only is a goal something that does not exist in your present moment, but the present-tense existence of a goal is a logical impossibility. A goal is a desired future result, something that you want to achieve at a point in time later than the present moment. Goals are not the same things as ambitions; they are the objects of ambitions, which can only be satisfied in the future. As the *Oxford English Dictionary* explains, a goal is the future end toward which your past or present behavior is directed; it is not that past or present behavior itself. Aristotle's *eudemonia* is something distant and remote, Freud's peaceful *stillness* is a form of future death, and Shakespeare's *venture* is pursued during all of the tomorrows that make up our course through life.

A goal, by definition and logical understanding, is never part of your current reality. How can it be? If your goal is to have a million dollars and you have a million dollars already, then that wealth is not a goal—it is just a statement about your current condition. If your goal is to weigh 150 pounds and you weigh that much right now, then having that healthy weight is not a goal. A goal must necessarily refer to and describe a state of affairs that does not exist, at least not yet. It is, at most, a sought-after future possibility. It cannot be an actual present-tense reality. Your goal, whatever it is, is the object of your wants and your desires. That is the only way that thinking about goal-setting makes any sense at all. A goal, to be totally candid about it, is nothing more than a wish: a wish that the future will be the way you want it to be.

When you watch the birthday child wish for a pony and then blow out the candles, do you really expect to hear tiny hoofbeats in the kitchen? When you wish upon a falling star, do you really force reality to obey your commands? If you cross your fingers before scratching off your lottery ticket, will you already be a winner?

No? Then why should our understanding of the goal-setting kind of wishes be different from those other kinds? If we don't expect positive expectations and a carefully stated desire to produce ponies out of birthday candles or futures out of falling stars, then we why do we expect them to produce life transformations out of cravings and goals?

The short answer to that question is that we allow ourselves to expect those things because it makes us feel good. It is comfortable and reassuring to believe that we can just wish, or goal-set, our way to a better life. When George and Lennie were sleeping on hay and straw in shabby bunkhouses, the thoughts of future farms and rabbits made the bunks seem a little less squalid. They were heartened that the expression of a wish for the future could make the future conform to that expression.

We are all like that to some degree, aren't we? We experience the dissatisfaction of the imperfect life we are living today—and remember that nobody's life is truly perfect—and we long for a tomorrow that comes closer to perfection. The belief that we can control the future by staking out our preferences and conjuring up an image is unrealistic, but it is delightful. It makes us feel warm and calm and it gives us peace. Most of all, it gives us a sense of power. It makes us feel as if we may actually be able to control the future. And everybody—everybody!—likes to feel powerful and in control.

It's easy to see how the belief in the power of goal-setting got to be so popular. Many writers, life coaches, self-help gurus, mystics, metaphysicians, and secret sharers have gotten rich by telling the world that the quickest path to self-improvement is the setting of appropriate goals. Decide what you want to change, they say, and the rest will fall into place. If you've read those books or heard those lectures you may remember slogans like, "If you don't know where you're going, any road will take you there," and "You have to know what target you're shooting at before you can hit a bull's-eye." And, lest we forget, "The difference between success and failure is nothing more than a well-defined goal." They remind us that a goal is the key to success at any task, that a proper diagnosis is half the cure, and that every successful business has a "mission statement."

Once you "know your goals," whatever that means, then Positive Thinking or the Law of Attraction or the Akashic Field or the Universal Mind or the Over-Soul or the 80/20 Rule will bring you what you want. Concentrate, meditate, ruminate. Believe and you will achieve. Shoot for the moon and land in the stars. Visualize to actualize. And so it goes, on and on and on. The true believers of creative visualization and goal-setting often take their cue from Marcus Aurelius, the second-century Roman emperor and Stoic philosopher whom they quote in support of their theory that we can change our circumstances and our future by thinking about goals. "Our life is what our thoughts make it," he wrote. That does sound pretty hopeful, and it certainly supports the theory that we can all believe to achieve. No one remembers, however, that Aurelius also preached that human lives are predetermined. Nothing we do, say, or think can change a single molecule of the life that we have been predestined to live. "Whatever happens to you has been waiting to happen since the beginning of time. The twining strands of fate wove both of them together: your own existence and the things that happen to you." I am not as skeptical as Aurelius when it comes to self-determination. I do not believe that "the twining strands of fate" wove our destiny at the dawn of time, but maybe I can convince you that creative visualization and its relatives are not enough to change the future. My first witness is Tom Dewey.

In November 1948 Harry Truman had been president of the United States for a little over three years. He presided over the American victories in World War II, supported the founding of the United Nations, rebuilt postwar Europe with the Marshall Plan, brought racial integration to the US Armed Forces, and recognized the newly established state of Israel. Nonetheless, and in spite of all of those achievements, when the 1948 election approached he was a distant second to the popular Republican governor of New York, Thomas E. Dewey. Truman's public approval ratings were underwater, and Dewey's election was viewed as a sure thing. Major public opinion survey organizations actually stopped polling altogether, thinking that there was no uncertainty worth measuring and nothing left to predict. Dewey was riding a high wave of confidence, the public's and his own. He could see that his election was in the bag—*he could just see it.*

Truman, though, never gave up. His famous Whistle Stop campaign traveled over 22,000 miles in two months. He spoke to large and small crowds, and like Dewey, he also visualized success. In speech after speech he laid out his vision for America and proclaimed hope and optimism. Three days before the election, he even told a crowd in St. Louis, Missouri, that he felt "sustained" by the country's popular support of his candidacy.

Popular support? Who was he kidding? Most political observers expected Truman to get crushed. One such creative visualizer of a Dewey presidency was the strongly Republican newspaper the *Chicago Tribune*. The *Tribune* was so sure of the power of this prediction that its editors set a banner headline "Dewey Defeats Truman" on the front page of its November 3, 1948, first edition, just before Truman clinched the presidency with 303 electoral votes.

How could that happen? Political experts all across the country had visualized a Dewey victory. Dewey visualized his own triumph. The editors of the *Tribune* not only visualized it, they manifested a sure faith in the power of thought by proclaiming their envisioned future in black-and-white newsprint and announced it as the news of the day.

Have you ever played football? Baseball? Tennis? Golf? Did your coach tell you that you should visualize your victory so that your goals would become reality? Guess what? The other team's coach was telling them the same thing. One of you learned the same hard lesson as Thomas Dewey, the *Chicago Tribune*, and everybody else who puts their faith in imaginative goal-setting: wishing doesn't really make it so.

If human beings really could imagine their futures into existence, then why would not every drowning sailor throughout history have simply visualized a timely rescue? Why should anyone still succumb to disease, poverty, plane crash, loss, misery, and despair when all it takes is a wish and a goal to defeat every bane of human existence? You already know why, don't you?

Here is another important thing to remember about goals: because their objects exist only in the future, having a goal cannot possibly change or improve your life in the present. If you intend to create your own Personal Renaissance *right now*, then you have to take some action *right now* that can change your circumstances *right now*. The future is not some pie-in-the-sky alternate reality universe that you reach through wishes and wormholes. It is made up of a million billion instantaneous, consecutive, present moments, a nearly infinite rush and roar of *now* moments one after another. Every individual molecule of immediacy is like one of the flashing rectangles that our passenger on *The Imaginary Train* looks at through the window. The passenger couldn't change the future directly, but he or she did change the present by deciding to stop the train. After that, the passenger allowed that newly changed present to extend itself into the future unceasingly with every step they took farther and farther away from the tracks. Once our passenger pulled Emergency Stop, that single act changed the present, and the newly formed present went on to re-create the future.

How can you achieve the same life-changing results? Not with goals certainly, because their uncertain future realization can't touch the present. Not with simple wishes, because they don't have the power to change reality. Not with visualization, manifestation, concentration, meditation, rumination, activation, the rule of thirds, crystal dynamism, inspiration, enthusiasm, string theory, your special secret, your imaginary friend, or the law of large numbers, because—well, just because none of them will work.

You certainly have the right to believe in whatever you want to, and if you decide to base your life on superstition or moonshine, that's up to you. But if you do that, I respectfully suggest that you will be disappointed with the results.

So what options does that leave us?

Around 500 BC, a Chinese military genius named Master Sun wrote a treatise called *The Art of War*. Master Sun, or Sun Tzu as he is usually known today, described the ways that wise generals fight battles and win wars. Over the years, *The Art of War* has been studied by military leaders and officers worldwide. Medieval Japanese generals credited its wisdom with letting them win battles without lifting a weapon. Douglas MacArthur was an avid fan. The US Army uses it in its libraries and training programs. So do the Marines. The Central

Intelligence Agency refers to it on its website's discussion of "Intelligence in War."

Nowadays, Sun Tzu's masterpiece has applications that range far beyond the study of battles and military conquest. It is studied in such diverse fields as commerce, office management, business practices, public relations, legal advocacy, sports, leadership training, negotiations, management, and even electronic gaming. What makes it so universally influential? And what makes it relevant to our own internal quest for Personal Renaissance? The answer comes from one of Sun Tzu's major feats of brilliance: his differentiation between strategy and tactics.

In Sun Tzu's world of wars and battles, *strategy* refers to the method of a military operation. *Tactics*, on the other hand, describe the step-by-step process that will accomplish that strategy. Both strategy and tactics serve the overarching aim of the military general who desires to win battles. To paraphrase Nietzsche, winning the battle is the object that the general would most love to achieve. If a general aims to win a particular battle by destroying the enemy's bridge, then bridge destruction is the strategy. Framing the strategy, however, is not nearly enough. How shall the general destroy the bridge? What steps will he or she take to carry out the strategy? What is the best way to reify the plan—to make it come true? The answers to those questions are the nuts-and-bolts work of tactics.

This terminology has been borrowed by the civilian world, which uses it in business, sports, and day-to-day life. If an automobile company wants to improve its market share by selling a lot of cars, then selling a lot of cars is its strategy. To actually accomplish that strategy, the company's tactics may include hiring the best engineers, figuring out what kind of cars people want, and then manufacturing those kinds of cars. If a basketball coach wants to reach the league championship, then winning the most games during the season would be a good strategy. To accomplish that strategy, the coach might use tactics such as designing effective plays, teaching good ball-handling techniques, and training his team members to perform as a cohesive unit.

If our general decides to destroy the enemy's bridge by having airplanes fly over and drop bombs on it, then airplane-flying and bomb-dropping are the tactics.

The general, the automaker, and the coach in these examples are all using strategies to implement their desires and tactics to carry out their strategies. But they also have something else in common—something that happens between the desire and the strategy they frame to achieve it. At the very instant they committed themselves to the achievement of the ends that they desired—win the battle, succeed in business, reach the playoffs—they each created something new in the world, a real-life condition that did not exist before that moment. They fashioned it from the raw material of their determination and they manufactured it out of the immediacy of their present tense. It was no mere goal—no anticipation of a future success that they wished would arrive at some later date.

The condition they created—the thing that changed their world at the moment of its creation—is called *resolve*.

Resolve precedes strategy, and it comes way before tactics. Once you recognize the inadequacy of your life right now, and after you identify the thing you love the most, then you have to develop a firm resolve to reify your Renaissance life. On that sunny June day in Florence when I resolved to improve my happiness by getting a PhD and giving up the practice of law, that act of resolution was as real, as immediate, as current, and as present tense as my heartbeat. It was not a wish for the future or something that I hoped to bring about at a later date. It was an actual here-and-now thing. It was a non-physical, mental thing for sure, but it was genuine and true and I possessed it in the immediacy of that moment. My resolve changed the reality of my time and place. It changed my very identity. I was no longer a dissatisfied lawyer who didn't know how to spend his remaining days. I may have been that before I walked out of the Piper's Thumb and crossed the threshold of my Life's Frontier into the Renaissance sunshine of Maria Novella, but my resolve changed all of that. After that I was something different. Instead of a disgruntled lawyer, I was an embryonic doctor of philosophy. An incipient college professor and writer. My resolve had rebirthed me as an agent of purpose. Right then and there.

You can and will change yourself and your world at the instant you develop a specific resolve. I'm not referring now to some kind of ethereal, translucent, spectral, or wishy-washy goal. Resolve is something far, far, different.

A goal may become actualized in the future or maybe not at all, but in either case it cannot inhabit the reality of *nowadays*. Resolve, on the other hand, always changes you *right now*. It becomes part of your real world at the instant you create it. From that instant in time it lives within you. There is nothing hypothetical or speculative about it. You don't have to wonder if it will exist someday or hope that it will come true when you blow out the candles. You can feel it with every thought you think and with every breath you take. It initializes your Personal Renaissance right then and there.

Think of the root meaning of the word *Renaissance*: *birth*. A newborn baby breathes a first breath right then and there. The baby does not put "first breath" on a to-do list. The mother does not set a goal for the baby to start breathing at some later date. The father does not write up an action plan for the baby's first breath. The midwife does not circle a date on the calendar so that everyone can be sure that the baby's first breath comes right on schedule.

No. The baby is born *now*. The baby starts breathing *now*. The baby's life has changed *now*. So has everyone else's. The baby's corner of the world has experienced an instantaneous Renaissance. It happened with the crashing immediacy of a brand-new life demanding attention and expressing a clear resolve to create a transformed world that did not exist before the baby raised his or her voice.

There can be a billion breaths in a single human life. Each one follows the last one and each one creates the next one, and on and on and on. They are as spontaneous and as immediate as—well, as breathing in and out. They extend the baby's life through childhood all the way to maturity and then into old age. But they all start with the first one. Each one follows and owes its currency to that one. The resolve of life begins with that first deliberate gulp that claims as much of the world's free air as it needs to change the universe.

Your own Renaissance life is much like that baby. It is born with your resolve, demanding your attention, creating its own new reality.

Simple goal-setting? Hardly.

Here is what I hope you will take away from this chapter. Your Personal Renaissance experience will happen in one single present moment. It will change your world right then and there, and the reality of that change will extend itself forward, rippling through, creating, and sustaining the next billion then-and-theres.

Resolve brings the dawning of creation.

SIXTH
GUIDEPOST

Resolve.

The Imaginary Train

The landscape slows down beyond the window. Eventually, but not all at once, the landscape stops speeding past and becomes calm. Calm and still. The tobogganing train car becomes silent. The steel screech has stopped. The train is still. You let go of the seat that was supporting you while you couldn't stand alone, and you take a halting step forward down the aisle. One single indecisive step in the direction of an open door and whatever lies beyond. A few more strides to the door, a few steps down, and there you are. Finally.

Outside the train.

CHAPTER 7

Reification, or Writing Your Script

"The strategist makes small things into big things."
Miyamoto Musashi

"How do you eat an elephant?"

You have probably heard that tired old riddle and its not-so-hilarious answer a thousand times.

"One bite at a time."

You may also remember the adage that a journey of a hundred miles begins with a single step. True enough. But what that adage doesn't mention is that after the first step there has to be a second one and a third one, and on and on and on like that for a hundred miles. Each and every step is incrementally necessary to get you to your destination, but every increment is small and partial. At any stage of your journey, it is possible to get lost.

To complete the hundred-mile journey, to finish eating the elephant, and to achieve the thing you love the most, you have to implement your strategy with effective tactics.

I am writing this chapter in the magnificent Main Reading Room of the National Library of Greece. Since arriving in Athens a month ago, I have spent many days in this amazing room, writing, reading, and thinking about the ancient wisdom contained within its walls. Twenty Ionic columns surround the reading area. Each one is about four feet across and thirty feet tall. The rectangle they form is nestled within the outer walls of the room, nineteen layers of bookshelves arranged in three tiers. There are catwalks at the second and third tiers, and they connect to a spiral staircase in each corner. Next door is Plato's Academy (not the ancient one, but the modern research institute of the same name) and the University of Athens.

In the mornings I take the subway from the Tissio station to Omonia Square and then carry my shoulder bag a kilometer down Panapistimio Street to the library. Today, like most days, lunch will be a salad at the Homestyle Café in the nearby park on Stadiou Street. By the time I leave for home, it will be dark and I will share the return trip with a thousand or so released office workers. Together, we daily cram the streets, coffee shops, and subway cars. I wander through the symphonies of lyric conversations.

Like libraries everywhere, the Reading Room has its share of eccentric regulars. An old lady sits in the back of the room and spends her days staring intently at the entrance as if she expects a horde of book thieves. She has worn the same mismatched pair of striped leggings every day for the last three weeks. Next to my favorite table sits a middle-aged man with shoulder-length unwashed hair. He has spent all of December, and probably much longer than that, searching through enormous folios of bound newspapers and scrawling miniature Greek letters in little square boxes that he draws on sheets of white paper. I can't tell if he is taking notes on a research project or just doodling. About five times every day he complains that I am typing too loudly on my laptop (I'm not). He expresses his displeasure by air-riffing his fingers on an imaginary keyboard and screwing up his face into an expression of disgust.

This library is famous for its fine collection of Greek antiquity, including the first publication of my favorite literary work, Homer's 3,000-year-old poem, *The Odyssey*. Homer's masterpiece tells the story of Odysseus and his return from the Trojan War. Odysseus devised the plan to build a huge wooden horse that the Trojans disastrously misinterpreted as a gift from the gods and dragged inside their walls. Sadly for them, the hollow structure was filled with warriors who spilled out while the Trojans slept. Thus did Odysseus conquer the city and win the war. That ploy, the famous "Trojan horse," cemented Odysseus's reputation among the ancient Greeks as the cagiest of all heroes. Homer himself calls him "the master of the land ways and the sea ways." The ancient stories of Greek mythology are chock-full of heroes who are bigger, stronger, and more powerful, but no one is smarter than Odysseus. When it comes to having ideas, he has no equal.

Therefore, it's a little surprising to find out that the poem bearing his name is mainly the story of the failures he encountered while returning to his home on the island of Ithaka. The return trip took him ten years longer than it should have, and it was filled with dreadful calamities that destroyed his ships, killed his crew, and nearly killed him as well. His sailors were drugged, eaten by cannibals, crushed by flying boulders, and turned into pigs. They died at the hands of monsters, giants, gods, and witches. The only common denominator in this catalog of disasters is that most of the deaths were the fault of Odysseus's bad planning.

Right. This genius of strategic planning couldn't sail a few ships on a peacetime cruise through the Mediterranean Sea to Ithaka without getting lost, blown off course, and shipwrecked. His homeward journey turned into a misery tour of the Mediterranean Rim, taking him thousands of miles off course to Italy, Tunisia, Spain, and pretty much every barren island and rocky upcropping between Asia and Gibraltar. When he finally did make it home, it was only because the kindhearted king of a distant island took pity on him and gave him a new ship and crew. But, true to his dismal record, Odysseus got them killed, too, and he ended up swimming to shore like the blundering castaway that he was.

And it gets worse. When he finally did get home, he found that his palace had been overrun by trespassers, his son was about to be murdered, and 104 no-good scoundrels were trying to force his wife to marry one of them. It took the goddess Athena to keep Odysseus from losing his kingdom, his son, and his wife, and then getting rubbed out by the lowlife brigade.

So here's the question: How did Odysseus go from being the master of the Trojan War to such an incompetent underachiever? Simple. Bad tactics.

If you were the hero of the Trojan War and you had resolved to get on with your life after years of battle, then returning home to your loving wife and son would be a pretty good strategy. That is what Odysseus thought, too, and he was right. His strategy was flawless, and his resolve was strong. His resolve to get back home changed him instantaneously from an aimless loiterer who was hanging around the scene of yesterday's battles into a homeward-bound hero, ready for the praise and adoration that he justly deserved. But even the strongest resolve and the wisest strategy need good tactics to succeed. And Odysseus's tactics were terrible.

Odysseus and his crew started out by insulting the god-king Zeus, who got even by stirring up hostile storms that sent them to the wrong end of Europe. After that, they got drunk on lotus leaves, some of them were eaten by one-eyed giants, the survivors wasted a magical bag of friendly winds, and for good measure they offended Zeus one more time. As if that wasn't enough, Odysseus and his dwindling crew also ran afoul of a sea witch, a six-headed rock-beast, and a whirlpool monster that ate ships.

Odysseus's resolve was to live happily ever after. His strategy was to get himself, his ships, and his sailors home as fast as he could. So far, so good. Nonetheless, he failed miserably. The story of his failure can teach us a very important lesson. Sometimes, often times, framing a good strategy is the easiest part of crossing the frontier. Odysseus knew what would make him happy; making it come true was the real chore. If you don't want your Renaissance to get eaten alive with Odysseus's crewmen, then you must remember this: a good strategy is not enough. You also need to develop a specific set of tactics that will efficiently advance that strategy and allow you to reify your resolve. Sun Tzu himself said that "strategy without tactics is the slowest road to victory."

One day not long ago I was talking to my friend Mike, who was dissatisfied with the condition of his life. In fact, he was almost at the edge of despair. He was struggling through divorce proceedings that seemed to be going nowhere. He had switched jobs for better pay, but his new boss turned out to be a scam artist who treated his employees unfairly. Before he realized how awful that new job would be, Mike had already moved to a new city and rented a nicer apartment, which he quickly discovered he could not afford because his income was less than he had expected. His personal life was also a mess, with a series of unsuccessful relationships, one after another. His financial situation was touch-and-go. His health was suffering, and his emotional well-being was shaky. His doctor had put him on antidepressants, but they didn't help very much and he couldn't afford the psychological therapy that he needed. Through all of this he tried to stay cheerful and positive, and he told me that my new life had inspired him to believe that he also could achieve a Personal Renaissance.

"That's great!" I encouraged him. "How are you going to do that?"

Mike smiled broadly and pulled a piece of paper out of his pocket. A to-do list. So far, so good—until he started reading. "Well," he began, "I really need to change jobs so I can make enough money to pay my rent so I'm going to check out some online job sites. I may go to community college and take some classes. Oh, plus I need new tires for my car and I'd really like to find a nice girlfriend." He put the list down. "I know that sounds like a lot," he sighed. Then he smiled again. "But I know I can get it done!"

A better job, a stable income, an education, and a fulfilling relationship are all good things, and if Mike succeeded in getting them he would almost certainly be happier. But seriously? With a list like that he was never going to get close to the place he wanted to be.

Looking at job sites? Which ones, and for what kind of job? I guess he would have defined a better job as one he liked that paid well. But that was a pretty wide-open field. Would he take a job as a coal miner or a brain surgeon? Probably not. Movie star? Astronaut? For sure. Good luck.

A college education could help improve his life, but that idea was no better than the job search. First, it was way too uncertain—"I *may* go back." Second, it was too vague. "Take *some* courses"? Why? Which ones? Why those? How would he pick them?

And as for his personal life, did he really think that he would find a "nice girlfriend" (what would make her "nice," by the way?) while his life was a shambles of poverty and depression?

I listened like a friend should listen and I tried to be encouraging. I wished him good luck and I meant it. That was almost a year ago, and Mike has not done any of the things he wanted to do. He is still in debt, and the divorce proceedings are still dragging on with no end in sight. He has moved from his old apartment into another one that he can't afford. He has found a new job, but he hates it so much that he's developed a bad attitude that gets him into trouble. There is an open-admission community college in his town, but he hasn't registered. He may have bought some new tires for his car, though, so I suppose that's a start.

If Mike had thought more clearly about his situation, he would have seen that his predicament really had only two parts—financial insecurity and a lack of personal fulfillment—and there were two basic reasons he was not going to succeed at fixing them: first, he had substituted ineffective goal-setting for a capable strategy, and second, his tactics were a mess.

Behavioral psychologists have discovered that in our day-to-day lives we all use facilities called *scripts*. These scripts are lists or sequences of deeds and actions that carry us from one situation to another. These sequences are usually informal and we often don't give them a second thought while using them, but they are incredibly important. Think about a play or a movie. The plot only hangs together and makes sense if the actors perform one line at a time and in the proper order. If they don't, then even a masterpiece by Shakespeare would be a mishmash of one confusing scene stumbling over another. It would make no sense because its script would no longer tell a story.

A recipe is a good example of a kind of script. If you want to make a salad for yourself and a friend, your script might be, "Buy the veggies, chop and cut, mix them up, add the dressing." If you resolved to prepare a banquet for a hundred guests, you would need a longer script, but the idea would be the same. First you do one thing, and then you do the next thing. You eat the elephant one bite at a time.

Just like the kind of script that actors use to perform their roles, your script will have a line that leads to another line that leads to another, all the way to the conclusion. If you perform the last line first and then the third and then the tenth and only then go back to the first, your story will fail. In the same way, each step of your path to Personal Renaissance must be taken in its own order, at its own proper time, neither too soon nor too late. There are usually a whole lot of things that you have to do to get from where you are to where you want to be. You can't skip a single one of them, and you can't do them out of order.

On November 26, 2011, a group of NASA scientists launched a rocket from Cape Canaveral, Florida. The rocket carried a strange-looking contraption called the Curiosity rover. It was about as big as a car but looked more like a giant mechanical spider. The scientists had resolved to send Curiosity to Mars, where it would land and study the planet. It would examine the environment, look for signs of life, and transmit its discoveries to an excited bunch of researchers back on Earth. Mars is our planetary neighbor in the solar system, but it's still pretty far away. Curiosity would have to travel 350 million miles to reach its Martian landing site, a spot called Gale Crater. To make matters more difficult, Mars circles the sun at a speed of about 54,000 miles per hour while Earth is traveling about 67,000 miles per hour in a different orbit. Landing a super-scientific exploration vehicle on Mars was a good strategy if you had resolved to learn about the planet, but your tactics had better be a little bit more detailed than that or else you would just end up with millions of dollars' worth of space junk and a lot of explaining to do. The NASA scientists and engineers had committed themselves to an elephant-sized project. If they had tried to swallow it whole, it would have choked them and strangled their chances for success. In order to nibble their elephant one bite at a time they needed a script with a lot of lines, a lot of individual, discrete steps.

If you are going to build a planetary rover, you need a careful design. But before you can design the vehicle, you have to study the terrain of its destination. There's no point in dropping a million-dollar dune buggy in the middle of a swampy patch of quicksand. But before you can study the terrain, you have to find (or build) a telescope that lets you see a patch of ground on a world millions of miles away. To get your spaceship where you want it to go, you have to calculate the relative orbits of two planets that are speeding away from each other at fantastic speeds, and then you have to figure out where your destination will be in the nine months it takes to get there. So first you have to learn the math that lets you plot the trajectory of your rocket ship. You have to decide when the rover should disengage from the rocket that carries it into outer space. But wait: before you can calculate any of those things, you have to measure the speeds at which everything is traveling, map out the planetary orbits, account for the effects of gravity and inertia and acceleration, and aim for the exact right position in the universe where you expect your landing spot to be when your rocket ship finally gets there. Between its launch on November 26, 2011, and its landing on August 6, 2012, Curiosity had flown over 350 million miles. Nonetheless, the scientists put it down less than two miles from the landing site they had chosen years before: a two-mile margin of error after a journey of 350 million miles to a spot of ground that had been zooming away at 54,000 miles an hour for nine months. When Curiosity landed at Gale Crater, its safe arrival represented the successful conclusion of thousands of individual steps and a thousand more separate decisions. It was a pretty impressive demonstration of the value of following a carefully written script

As I am writing this chapter—and probably as you are reading it, too—the Curiosity rover is sending Earthbound scientists a wealth of information about a world where no human being has ever set foot. Those scientists who once created a monumental resolve for themselves crossed millions of miles of barren space and landed the rover carefully enough that every one of its fragile parts worked flawlessly. They had looked through the blurry window of their Earthbound train and pulled the Emergency Stop on human ignorance. They took one step and then another, and then they wandered freely through the universe. Because they did, humanity has learned things about that universe that no one would have been able to see from a comfortable seat in a speeding carriage. It may have been 350 million miles to Gale Crater, but it was worth the trip.

Your journey may not be as far—physically—as the voyage of Curiosity, but if you have picked a worthy destination for yourself, it's far enough to require some careful planning. Any Personal Renaissance is far enough from where you are sitting right now that in order to get there you will need tactics. It would be nice if you could get a preprinted roadmap to your destination, but believe me, there is no such thing. Internet mapping sites and GPS units are no good for what lies ahead of you. That means that before you get started, *you have to draw your own map.* You have to rely on your own vision.

SEVENTH GUIDEPOST

You need tactics
to fulfill your strategy.

The Imaginary Train

You are outside the train car now. You have removed yourself from the comfort and protection of the carriage and, instead, you are standing all alone. Exposed. Solitary and disconnected from the rush and roar of the machine. As alone and as new as a butterfly fresh from its cocoon. Confined by nothing and all at once enveloped by the universe. Encircled but not enclosed, surrounded by your new exposure to completeness.

The sunlight is warm and the breeze is cool as you walk around. You hear the wind waving the trees and the water of a stream somewhere as it passes over rocks and rapids. The autumn greens are turning red, and leaves are floating deliberately to the ground. The sky is clear. The grass is high, and it receives your footsteps as you wade through it. It acknowledges your progress and then returns to itself. Everything belongs where it is. Including you.

CHAPTER 8

YOUR MOVING FRONTIER

"Take time to deliberate,
but when the time for action comes,
stop thinking and go in."

NAPOLEON BONAPARTE

When I walked into the Piazza of Santa Maria and resolved to exchange an unfulfilling career for the one I would love the most, that was a big step. But it was just the first step. I knew that I was going to change my life—indeed, I had done so already simply by creating my resolve. I felt that my timing was right because my children had reached places in their lives where they were headed for financial self-sufficiency. Next, I developed a strategy for implementing my career-aimed resolve—graduate school, a doctorate, and teaching. But how was I going to make all of that happen? I needed a script. A map. Tactics.

Here's how I proceeded to eat my elephant. It was a process of steps and stages, and it often went much slower than I wanted it to. Some of the steps were hard, some were fun, all were necessary. I am not suggesting that you retrace my steps on your own path to Personal Renaissance. Your destination will be different than mine, and so your steps will be different than mine. But hearing about the tactics that worked for me may give you some helpful pointers when you start planning your own journey. Furthermore, it demonstrates that with each step I took, with each line of script I performed, I moved my frontier a little further away from my past and a little bit closer to my Renaissance. As I pushed westward (so to speak), the unknown hinterlands in front of me shrank and became less threatening, less overwhelming, and less unknown. My tenacity tamed the wilderness of an uncertain future. Yours will, too.

Here is how I wrote and acted out my script.

Since I had decided that I needed a graduate school degree, I had to pick my field and my school. I knew that the Pennsylvania State University had a branch campus near Harrisburg and that it offered a doctorate in American studies. I figured that nothing was more American than the US Constitution, which I had worked with for the last thirty-some years. The subject seemed like a good fit, and the school was conveniently located. I decided that I would pursue a doctorate in American studies from Penn State.

Next I had to determine if that decision was realistic. That was not something I could completely figure out on my own, but I could examine my decision for any obvious roadblocks. I saw two possibilities. First, I was fifty-eight. I didn't feel that my age was an issue (obviously) but someone else might, and if that someone was the person who would decide to accept or reject my application, I wanted to know about it in advance. Second, I wanted a doctoral degree, but I didn't have a master's degree. I knew that a PhD program traditionally required a master's for admission, but getting that degree would take about two more years and I wanted to avoid that additional time expenditure if I could.

After doing that self-examination, I sent an email to a judge I knew in Harrisburg who was, I knew, acquainted with one of the senior American studies professors at Penn State. If anyone could answer my questions, it would be him, so I asked my friend to arrange a meeting. I was still in Italy when I sent that email, but by the time I got home we were all set. A few days later the three of us sat down for a light snack and a conversation about my future.

That meeting convinced me that my age would not be an issue and that I could submit an application without a master's degree. The next step was finding out how to apply to graduate school. It turned out that this was an elaborate process all by itself. I had to take and pass a standardized test called the Graduate Record Exam (GRE). I had to complete a lengthy, detailed application. I had to assemble all of my college grade transcripts, which meant that I would have to get my college and law school to dig my files out of old archives, certify them, and send them to Penn State. I hoped that those records were still available, but I wasn't sure. I also needed three letters of recommendation from former professors. I tried to have that requirement waived on the grounds that I hadn't had a teacher in over thirty years, but rules are rules and so I had to hunt up old professors who would remember me (and still be alive). Then I had to write an admissions statement that explained why I should be accepted, why I wanted a doctorate, and what I would do with it after graduation.

I knew that this would be a difficult and time-consuming process, and I was still a practicing attorney with a busy schedule. So I decided I had to take care of that first.

Before I resigned my position with the law firm and closed my practice, I wanted to be very certain I was on the right course. I arranged to attend some seminar classes for American studies graduate students. I spoke to students who were already enrolled in the program and asked them some questions that were important to me. I researched the PhD program in the Penn State academic catalog to learn the requirements for the degree. How many courses would I need to complete? How many could I take each semester? What kind of tests would I have to pass? What kind of research papers would I have to write? How much would it cost? Finally, I spoke to some professors to get an idea of what it felt like to have a PhD in American studies. Was it something that I would like? And, most importantly, was it worth the effort? I wasn't going to be discouraged (again) by warnings about a soft job market. I just wanted to talk to people who had done the thing I was considering and find out if they were happy.

Businesspeople and investors call this kind of precommitment research "doing due diligence," and so I was doing mine. My due diligence told me that an American studies PhD was indeed worthy of my resolve. The law firm was next.

Disconnecting from the firm and from the practice of law was a multifaceted process. Many of the lawyers in the firm had been my friends for decades, and so I wanted to settle our business, legal, and financial relationships without any hard feelings. Breakups among lawyers can be very contentious and unpleasant. After all, everyone involved is a lawyer, we don't shy away from conflict, we know our rights, and we don't like to feel slighted. Lawsuits are frequent. Bad blood is common.

In spite of all that, our separation was civil and friendly. We tied up all of our financial loose ends and agreed on terms for me to continue having a relationship with the firm. Two of my former law students were starting their own law firm, so I sold one of them my beautiful barrister's desk. I had counseled thousands of clients across that desk, listening to their troubles and solving their problems. Turning it over to someone whose career I had helped start felt just right. I told my clients and colleagues that I was leaving, and then I was finished. For the first time in thirty-four years I did not have a law office to go to in the morning.

It was time to get busy on that application.

The GRE is a famously difficult test, and I knew that I couldn't just walk into a test center one day with no preparation and pass it. I took some online sample tests and bought an instructional book, but after several weeks of study I was still getting terrible scores on the practice tests. My daughter, the recent college graduate, had just aced the Law School Admissions Test. She recommended the company whose test prep materials she had used, and I found out that they also published books to prepare for the GRE. I bought one, studied some more, finally passed a few practice tests, and I then felt that I was ready to schedule the actual test. The book that my daughter recommended was worth its weight in gold, and I sailed through the GRE with one of the highest possible scores. Maybe I could be a graduate student after all.

The next step was writing my admissions statement, and I had exactly zero idea what it was supposed to say. My son had just finished his own graduate school career, so I asked him for ideas. Then I contacted one of my nephews, an American history professor, who agreed to review the finished product. Really, the admissions statement was simply a document of advocacy—I was making a case for why Penn State should accept me into its graduate school. I had been making cases on behalf of clients for a long time. Now I was advocating on my own behalf.

The rest of the applications process went smoothly. My colleges did indeed have my grade reports on file. I was able to find some professors who agreed to write the recommendations I needed. The online application was long but not difficult. Once I submitted everything to the graduate school, there was nothing for me to do but wait for the decision.

Several weeks later, I found out that I had been accepted. It was now officially crunch time. In the next few months I would have to finish some legal business, including the defense of a very complicated murder case. I had to schedule meetings with my academic adviser, plan my curriculum, arrange my classes, and buy my books. My son told me that all graduate students need a denim shirt and a messenger bag, so I had to buy those, too.

The day before the start of the fall semester, I attended a welcoming ceremony for new students. The faculty entered the hall in a formal procession with full regalia—academic gowns, caps, and hoods. As I was standing with the crowd, the chairman of our department saw me, and as he passed by he called out, "Welcome home." And that was exactly how I felt. Home.

I attended my first graduate seminar on August 27: Theory and Methods in American Studies. Over the next two years I attended about 800 hours of class sessions and wrote over a dozen long research papers. At the end of my first year, I took a test called the Candidacy Exam. The next year, I took a weeklong take-home exam called the Comprehensives. I had to pass both of them before I could write my doctoral dissertation. I finished the dissertation in the spring of my third year and defended it in May. The oral defense of a doctoral dissertation is an intense and grueling session where the candidate is grilled by four seasoned professors who have gone over the paper with a fine-tooth comb, searching for errors, logical inconsistencies, and faulty theories. No one who has defended a dissertation will ever forget the experience.

A few weeks later, my kids were in the audience at Penn State's Bryce Jordan Center in University Park, Pennsylvania, to watch the president of the university shake my hand and say, "Congratulations, Doctor," as I received my diploma. I may have been walking across a graduation stage, but I was really crossing my Life's Frontier. It was a very good day.

What had it taken to get to that very good day? From Florence to graduation was forty-nine months. During that time I planned to completion dozens of individual steps. I attended hundreds of classes, made thousands of decisions, read tens of thousands of pages of textbooks and research papers, and wrote at least a thousand pages of independent research. Looking back on my own forty-nine-month-long script, what lessons might there be for you?

First, I had dissected the problem into its smallest logical components. I didn't say, for example, "I will apply to graduate school." That step alone involved at least twenty-five individual, bite-sized increments. They started with deciding on a school, and they progressed all the way to completing the admission application. They were small increments, but they were not too small and they were realistic. I didn't let my planning get ahead of itself. If, for example, I had tried to decide in advance that when I took the GRE I would answer question number 29 with "B" or that during my third semester I would always raise my hand on Tuesday, that kind of micromanagement of future events would have been ridiculous and counterproductive. The tactical steps that I developed were realistic, they made sense, and they had enough specificity to produce results but not so much that they slowed me down. They were manageable, and they worked. The next three years contained some decisions that I made before school started and others that I modified as I progressed from one step to the next. That is what tactical thinking is all about.

Do you remember Mike, my friend who needed a new job? His tactics to improve his finances had one vague, imprecise, meaningless, and unproductive step—try to find a job online. His tactics for finding a nice girlfriend had even fewer steps—zero; he just wanted to find one. That is why I knew that he could never succeed. Achieving financial stability and forming a rewarding relationship can both be elephant-sized tasks, and without good tactics the only thing you'll swallow is disappointment. His script for financial security, for example, should have had dozens of lines. Explore the job market. Reach out to friends with jobs. Assess your job skills. Anticipate a need for retraining. Locate training opportunities. Evaluate potential sources of employment satisfaction. Determine what salary range is possible. Calculate a budget within that range. Specify a portion of the budget for rent. Search for affordable apartments. I could go on, but the point is that there are a lot of steps between a complex problem and a suitable solution. Mike wasn't nibbling at his problems one bite at a time. He was trying to eat the whole elephant in one big gulp, and when he realized that it wouldn't fit in his mouth all at once, he just gave up.

Next, I relied on my family and friends for help whenever I could. My son advised me about graduate school. My daughter told me about the best GRE practice book. My nephew reviewed my application letter. My judge friend introduced me to the senior professor. You should do the same thing. You have spent your whole life up to now meeting people and developing relationships. There is nothing lazy or underhanded about asking for help and nothing wrong with accepting the help of people who want to help you. I'm not talking about coercion or bribery, and I'm not talking about taking unfair advantage of people who may feel beholden to you. Here is the test I recommend to be sure that you are behaving fairly and appropriately: If there is a person for whom you would gladly perform a valuable service they asked of you, then it's okay for you to ask the same of them. Once. Don't be a pest about it.

Finally, in order to achieve my Personal Renaissance, I used the talents and abilities that I already had. I knew how to advocate, so I could write my application letter and advocate for myself. I knew how to write persuasively, so I could compose excellent term papers for my classes. I knew how to manage big projects, so organizing my dissertation was not as hard for me as it may have been for some others. I was accustomed to speaking in courtrooms, so speaking in classrooms was not much of a stretch.

You can do the same thing, no matter what your Personal Renaissance entails. Are you a real estate salesperson whose First Blank involves becoming a commercial artist? You already know how to appeal to the good taste of the buying public. You know how to market yourself and you have contacts in the community. You can use those advantages in art as well as in real estate. Are you a bookkeeper who would love to be a chef? You already know how to pay attention to details. You can estimate costs and keep track of expenses. You are familiar with business practices and you understand the value of reliability and precision.

The real estate salesperson and the bookkeeper in those examples have one thing in common with me: we each took

Nietzsche's advice and selected a Personal Renaissance based on something we love. The would-be artist loves art; the chef-to-be loves food. This is important because your passion for the thing you love will carry you over many hurdles when the path gets rocky. Your resolve will arise from adversity, but as it rises it must exemplify the thing you love the most and it must express your essential individuality. When you choose your Renaissance destination, you must pick one that is in line with the passion you carry with you. Odysseus wanted to return to his own home, not to anyone else's. Grandma Moses wanted to paint farm scenes, not Roman vases. I wanted to learn and teach, but I was not going to pick a subject that I would hate. American studies fit me like a glove. Lion-taming? Bomb-making? Self-mutilation? Not so much. I enjoyed every day I was in a classroom or a library or a lecture hall (no kidding). That's what it should be like for you, too. Allow your Personal Renaissance journey to bring you pleasure. Make it fun. Don't take shortcuts. Be grateful for every step. My steps took me to the classroom. Yours will probably take you someplace else. When you get there, it will seem new, familiar, strange, and wonderful all at the same time.

EIGHTH GUIDEPOST

You are the star
of your own script.
Make it a good one.

PART THREE

Peril

"In this advance, the Frontier is the outer edge of the wave — the meeting point between savagery and civilization.
FREDERICK JACKSON TURNER

INTRODUCTION

In 1960 the junior senator from Massachusetts had just turned forty-three years old when he accepted his party's nomination for president. John F. Kennedy was a naval officer and a Pulitzer Prize–winning best-selling author. He was charming, handsome, and rich, the son of one of America's wealthiest families and a decorated war hero. In 1943 Navy secretary James Forrestal had awarded Kennedy the Navy and Marine Corps Medal, praising the "outstanding courage, endurance and leadership" he demonstrated while saving the lives of his crew when their ship was blown apart. Kennedy had beaten back challenges from more seasoned politicians—his future running mate, Lyndon Johnson, among them—before receiving the Democratic Party nomination in Los Angeles on July 13. Two days later he gave the speech of a lifetime.

Kennedy understood the challenges that faced America and the world as he spoke in Los Angeles that summer. Political repression, poverty, and disease spread around the globe. Communist regimes threatened American interests in Asia, the Middle East, and the Caribbean. Crime, overpopulation, racism, and urban blight threatened American values at home. In the midst of an increasingly angry Cold War, nuclear devastation was never further away than one miscalculation. The world was listening to Kennedy that day, and he must certainly have felt the weight of the future and of fate. He spoke of opportunities and of perils. He called his speech, "The New Frontier."

The optimistic Kennedy recognized the New Frontier as a place of "unknown opportunities" and "unfilled hopes." It rewarded the pioneer who was "young at heart" and "stout in spirit." It decorated "imagination and courage and perseverance." But for all of its attraction, the New Frontier was filled with "hazards" and "hardships," and nothing could guarantee success. Even champions sometimes fail, after all. Even heroes lose their way. The path ahead was "uncharted," and the journey demanded courage. The risk of the unknown would not be placated by the "safe mediocrity of the past." He exhorted his fellow citizens to emulate previous pathfinders who had blazed trails and conquered peril by risking safety and comfort. The big question for Kennedy—"the question of the New Frontier"—was simply this: "Have we the nerve and the will?"

If all of that sounded risky, said Kennedy, it was—but there was no alternative. The future may bring doubts and reservations, but it arrives unbidden and cannot be held at bay. "The New Frontier is here whether we seek it or not," he warned.

Kennedy urged his listeners to draw the line between yesterday and tomorrow with courage and with hope. But make no doubt about it, he cautioned. There are perils.

The Imaginary Train

As you walk away from the place where you stopped the speeding train, you become aware that you have lost your sense of distance and of time. You turn around to look behind you and you are surprised to find that the train and the tracks are nowhere to be seen. For a moment you actually think about finding them, waiting for the train to return, standing still until it does, and then getting back on the carriage. Maybe you can retrace your steps and listen for the sound of the rails. But that idea passes in a heartbeat. In a crystalline flash of immediacy the train and track are gone from your reality. They are no longer part of your life, and that realization, all by itself, has changed you into someone new. You are no longer their passenger. You rode them long enough. They brought you to this place, but now that's finished and you are finished with them.

You take another step, and then another. The horizon is far ahead of you, and you may not make it that far. But you take your first step right now and you continue to walk forward, not backward, nonetheless.

CHAPTER 9

SURVIVING ASGAARD

*"Criticism is something we can
avoid easily by saying nothing, doing
nothing, and being nothing."*

ARISTOTLE

Let's take stock of how far we've come. You have allowed yourself to recognize the incompleteness of your present condition, and like Grandma Moses you have created resolve out of adversity. You are ready to pull an Emergency Stop on your old unfulfilling life and walk away from the carriage that has conveyed you through a partial and inauthentic life. You have filled in your First Blank with the Nietzschean thing you love the most. You have set upon a strategy to create a Personal Renaissance from your resolve, and you have started to write the script of tactical steps that will reify your dream. Like Siddhartha, you have traded complacency for existential achievement. Like Odysseus, you have set your destination and are determined to reach it. And you look forward to being able to declare, like Edmund Hillary, that you are among the fortunate few who have had a dream and made it come true. In other words, you have embarked on a path that will carry you over your Life's Frontier.

So I guess that's all there is to it. Once you get off your train and chart your course, you can totally expect smooth sailing from there on in. In fact, everyone in the world will join hands with you, leading you on, helping you at every step, making sure that you never fall or stumble. Most of all, you will never hear a word of discouragement or despair, and no one will ever criticize you for the decisions you have made. Right? Hardly.

Knute Rockne once famously observed that when the going gets tough, the tough get going. Knute was one of the greatest football coaches of all time, and his Notre Dame dynasty teams won 105 games and five national championships. He probably knew a few things about being tough. But sometimes we have to turn his celebrated advice inside out for it to make better sense.

When the tough get going, that's often when the going really gets tough.

What do I mean? Simply this: Once you get started on your Renaissance journey, you can find yourself imperiled from the most unlikely places. You may be resolute and determined to achieve success, but that won't happen until you surmount the final challenge. The pre-Renaissance Dark Ages won't stay dead without a fight, and as President Kennedy warned us, the Frontier is filled with risks and dangers demanding to be overcome. During the historical Renaissance, Shakespeare called those dangers "the slings and arrows of outrageous fortune." You'll find them coming at you in your Personal Renaissance as well. And make no mistake about it: If you don't get ready for them, they can stop you dead in your tracks.

To get a better handle on this problem, let's look at a very old story from the time and land of the Vikings.

The cosmos of the Norse legends arose from a collision of ice and fire, and the gods built Nine Worlds from the body of a frost-giant. The divine land of Asgaard was connected to the human land of Midgaard by a bridge made of rainbows. The affairs of gods and humans were bound together in the branches of a titanic world-tree, and the king-god Odin ruled over everything. The Norse tales that have come down to us depict a rough-and-tumble universe filled with giants, monsters, struggles, and death.

Much of the rough tumbling in these stories comes from the elf-god Loki, who seems to exist solely to make trouble. Some scholars believe that he is thematically related to the devil Lucifer; both names may derive from an common etymological ancestor. In any event, Loki, like other fiends and demons, creates pain and suffering wherever he goes. His most famous outrage concerns the god-prince Baldur.

Baldur was the son of Odin and the goddess Frigg. He was the darling of Asgaard, adored by one and all. Legends say that he was the most beautiful, the gentlest, and the wisest of all the Norse gods. Some stories even say that he glowed with light and grace.

Because everyone loved Baldur, everyone was shocked when he started dreaming about his own murder. Odin was terrified and traveled to the foggiest outskirts of Asgaard to ask the monstrous goddess of death, Hel, for help solving the mystery of Baldur's dream. Hel gave Odin his answer, but it didn't make any sense. She prophesied that Baldur's dream would come true. He would indeed be murdered, and his brother Hod would be the one to kill him. Hod? *No way*, thought Odin. Hod was as gentle as Baldur, and there was no bad blood between them. Furthermore, Hod was blind and Baldur was a warrior. Certainly Hod posed no danger to the wisest god of all.

Nonetheless, a prophecy is a prophecy. So in order to prevent her son's death, Baldur's mother, Frigg, traveled to every land in the Nine Worlds and made everyone and everything promise that they would never harm Baldur. And when I say everything, I mean *everything*. She got promises from the trees, the stones, the rivers, and the oceans. Wind, fire, iron, earth, and every other form of matter all swore oaths not to hurt Frigg's son. When she finally returned from her mission she was satisfied that Baldur was safe from any danger. After all, how could he be killed if nothing in the universe was allowed to hurt him? The gods were so certain of his invulnerability that they invented a new sport: they started throwing things at Baldur and watched everything bounce harmlessly off his body. Everyone was having a great old time until Loki decided to put a stop to all the fun.

Loki found out that Frigg had forgotten to ask one thing for the usual promises. She had bypassed a tiny little bush that grew on the western edge of Asgaard. It was called mistletoe, and she thought that it was too frail to pose any danger to a god. When Loki heard this, he pulled a branch off of the mistletoe bush, whittled it down to a sharp point, and fashioned a deadly arrow. He knew Hel's prophecy that Hod would be his brother's killer, so he found the blind god and convinced him to join in the fun of throwing things at Baldur. With Loki to guide his hand, Hod cast the arrow straight at his brother's heart. The dream and prophecy had come true. Baldur fell to the ground and died.

The story of Baldur and the mistletoe can teach us a few valuable lessons about life on the frontier.

First of all, do you have a lot of friends? A solid support system? Family and relatives who love you? Plenty of people who will cheer you on, applaud your efforts, and celebrate your successes? If so, that's great. You should enjoy each and every one of them and be sure to accept all of the help and encouragement you can get. If you remember the description of my own tactical script, then you will recall that I asked for the help of my friends and family and I was lucky and happy to get it. Having people who love and support you will make your journey easier and more fun. We all need encouragement, applause, and approval. The New Testament even says that St. Paul commends his reader to enjoy the "great cloud of witnesses" that helps every seeker stay on the right path. So it is for all of us. Friends and supporters are great, and we should nurture and enjoy as many of them as we can get.

But we must also be aware that not everyone is enthusiastically longing to help us. Baldur had it better than we do; in fact, he had it better than anybody does. I know that not everyone on earth loves me, and I doubt if they all love you either. I am also willing to bet that neither of us radiates divine light. Gods and men, goddesses and women, every object on the lands and seas adored Baldur. Nonetheless, even he fell victim to a surprising attack from an unexpected direction.

Baldur's story illustrates an important point that we should remember as we go about creating our Renaissance lives. It's as simple as this:

As you move from resolve to Renaissance, there will be some people who won't support you.

I don't think that anybody is going to try to pierce your heart with a real-life deadly arrow (at least I hope not). I am talking about criticism and condemnation. Verbal arrows. Wounding words. Harmful negativity. These attacks may come at you from places that you didn't expect, and they will have a potency that you might not anticipate. Some people (like the gamers of Asgaard) will shoot their arrows at you for fun, all the time believing that their words are harmless, or even helpful. Others (like Loki) will aim straight for your heart with bad intent.

Whom do I mean? Well, people who have always resented you, for sure. Forget about tossing a sprig of mistletoe at you. You can count on those critics to throw everything at you but the kitchen sink. You know who they are, and their hostility should not come as a surprise. The surprises will come when other people—friends and those whom you like and respect—start bombarding you with the slings and arrows of outrageous fortune. You should count on most of these arrows coming from one of four sources.

First are the *Know-It-Alls*. These people claim, rightly or wrongly, to know everything about the life you want to achieve and they are glad to give you a masterclass about why you are doomed to fail. They are the avatars of The Second Blank ("That simply isn't possible because _____"). Let me give you a real-life example.

I was enjoying my first year of graduate school: happy to be reading good books, savoring the discussions in my seminar classes, finding my own insights, and generally having a wonderful time. When people asked me what I was going to do next, after I earned my doctorate, I would explain that I wanted to teach. Do some writing. Travel. "But first things first," I would always say. "First I have to finish my degree."

One evening at a party, I was approached by a man whom I knew only slightly. He told me that he had heard about my return to school. This guy was, by coincidence, the president of a local college. As someone who had devoted his life to higher education, he explained that he was thrilled to learn that I had gone back to school to obtain an advanced degree. "That's great," he gushed. "Fantastic! Wonderful! I can't tell you how terrific I think that is. I wish more people would do what you're doing." I smiled and waited for The Question. I didn't have to wait long. "What are you going to do next?"

I gave him my usual answer. "Who knows? I don't even have my degree yet. Write. Travel. And I would like to do some college teaching."

His eyes got big. "College teaching?" He sort of grimaced. "Forget it. Never going to happen."

Oh, really. "Why not?" I asked.

"Listen, Spero. I've spent the last thirty years of my life hiring college faculty, and I can tell you for a fact that nobody is going to hire a sixty-year-old beginning professor. Never going to happen."

He didn't say it with deliberate cruelty, but his antagonism for my resolve was obvious. He acted as if he was doing me a favor by telling me something I needed to hear. Like, "Spero, it's raining out. You'd better bring an umbrella." Or, "Spero, you're about to walk off a cliff. You'd better watch your step." What he actually did say was, "Spero, colleges and universities hire promising *young* professors who can be expected to make contributions to academia and science over the long term. Not old guys like us. Enjoy the party." And then he went off to mingle with someone else.

I had heard similar warnings from other Know-It-Alls, but his was the most direct. I spent a moment standing there and wondering after he had walked away. *Was he right? Was I wasting my time? Had I made a dreadful mistake? Was I chasing a hopeless dream?* To put it another way, *Should I have stayed on the safe and sheltered Lawyers' Train?* At least there I had a certain place, my seat was guaranteed, and no one could tell me that I didn't belong, or that I was too old or not good enough. Maybe I should never have pulled Emergency Stop.

Yeah, I wondered about those things for a moment—but only a moment.

Then I smiled and realized that he knew nothing about my resolve. He didn't know where I was coming from or where I wanted to go or how I intended to get there. His ideas of teaching were frozen solid by thirty years in the same place. He had hired professors, he had evaluated professors, he had been a professor, and he associated with professors. His idea of teaching was fixed by his own experience and aspirations, and that experience had nothing whatsoever to do with me.

As I came to learn, college professors have a certain professional pathway. It actually has a name: "the tenure track." To succeed on that track, they have to publish articles, attend conferences, go to meetings, be thought of as smart, and become well-known as competent (if not distinguished) scholars. There is nothing wrong with that track or with anyone who wants to be there. My college president acquaintance was right. The academic community populated its tenure track by making young PhDs and then training them how to publish articles, attend conferences, and go to meetings. Pretty soon, they would be thought of as smart and become well-known as competent (if not distinguished) scholars. Wait for next year's crop of PhDs and repeat. Then repeat again.

As I write this chapter, I am waiting for my spring semester to begin. I will be teaching three different courses at three different colleges. I am on nobody's tenure track. Instead, I have managed to stay on my own course. I don't go to meetings or attend conferences that don't interest me, and I don't write or publish anything that anyone else has chosen for me. Instead, I do the thing I love—teach students. I don't need a committee or a tenure track or a title to do that. My friend was right. At sixty years old I might not find a place on the tenure track. No problem. I don't need another version of the *clackety-clack-clack* I just got away from. My friendly Know-It-All had the razor-sharp vision of a man who had been looking out of the same little rectangular train window for his whole life and who couldn't see that there was a righteous frontier of adventure on the other side of Emergency Stop. His vision was keen, but his perspective was narrow. Because my path was outside his field of view, he couldn't see it. His reflection on the blurry window of his own carriage distorted his impressions of the outside world. He only knew his train.

NINTH GUIDEPOST

Beware the Know-It-Alls who condemn your resolve.

CHAPTER 10

SETTLERS AND MORALIZERS

*"Do not go where the path may lead,
go instead where there is no path
and leave a trail."*

HENRY DAVID THOREAU

The next variety of arrow throwers you should watch out for don't care what kind of life you are trying to create for yourself: they simply want to criticize you for abandoning the one that you are leaving behind. I had to deal with so many of these people that I came to divide them into two separate categories: the *Settlers* and the *Moralizers*.

First, let's talk about the Settlers.

The Settlers have worked hard to find a place on the train that you have resolved to leave, and they are determined to remain settled in their comfortable berth in their comfortable passenger car. They may not know about your Personal Renaissance and they won't usually care to learn too much about it. They already know about what you are leaving behind and they will view your resolve as silly—even threatening. They will pretend not to understand what you are doing or why. You will know them by their question.

"You're doing what?"

I wish I could tell you how many times I heard that question before I realized that it was not really a request for information but an expression of shock and disdain. In most cases, the person asking that question will have worked hard to achieve the status that you are deliberately throwing away. In my case, I heard, *"You're doing what?"* from most of the lawyers I knew. These were highly accomplished men and women who had studied for many long years, worked hard, fought to get ahead, clawed their way up the ladder of success, and reached the top of their profession. It would have taken a dynamite charge and a forty-mule team to get them to abandon their spot at the top of their pyramid, and when I told them that I was voluntarily leaving the very same spot that they had struggled to attain, and in many cases a higher and more desirable spot—well, you can't blame them for being confused.

The thing to remember is that the confusion of others is not a threat to you all by itself, but it can weaken your resolve if you're not ready for it. "Why would you want to turn your back on everything you've achieved? Don't you see how good we have it? Are you sure that you are making a smart decision?"

There are two things to know in order to dodge this arrow. First, the person who asks, *"You're doing what?"* is not trying to understand you or to convince you of anything at all—whether to stay or go, remain or change. Unless such people really and truly care deeply about what's in your best interests, they are instead trying to convince *themselves* that you have lost your marbles. If they can do that, they can feel better about their own decision to stay settled right where they are.

If you are crazy to turn your back on what you (and they) already have, then they must be smart to hold on to it. The craziness of your decision defends the saneness of theirs. *"You're doing what?"* is just another way of saying, "I'm smarter than you are."

The second thing to know is that the person who doesn't applaud your resolve for a Personal Renaissance may be correct—from his or her own perspective. After all, you didn't form that resolve until now. That other person may be just behind you in terms of the schedule of their decision-making. Maybe they haven't seen the Emergency Stop yet, maybe they haven't gotten brave enough to pull the handle, or maybe they just like being on the train. Some people belong where accident has planted them, and you may be talking to such a person. The person who questions your resolve and chooses instead to remain settled may be doing what is right for himself or herself, but you have to be careful to remember that that does not mean that their decision is right for you.

The Know-It-Alls and the Settlers may all be shooting arrows of negativity and discouragement at you, but their attacks are *pragmatic*. They believe (or at least they pretend to believe) that you are either logically wrong—your resolve makes no sense—or that you are dangerously wrong—you are going to hurt someone, probably yourself. The harder arrows to dodge come from the third category of mistletoe shooter: the Moralizer. This person will reluctantly (or sometimes enthusiastically) tell you that your conduct is morally wrong, that you are behaving unethically, maybe even sinfully, and that you should knock it off in order to preserve your integrity and your own virtue.

Remember that when I started telling my lawyer friends that I was going back to school, some of them complained that

I had no right to quit my practice when there was still so much injustice in the world. They knew that there might be some cases that no one else would touch, so some people with serious needs would never get the help they deserved. I was placing my personal whims above the needs of the community, they said. I was ignoring the interests of justice. These were serious accusations, and I took them as such. The bottom line was that I was being selfish.

One of my dearest friends, a distinguished scientist, felt the same way. "Just think of all the good things you can do as a lawyer, all the people you can help every day," she urged. "There's no way to do that in the academic world." She expressed her views with kindness, but her moralistic opposition to my resolve came through loud and clear.

We all want to think of ourselves as people of honor and decency. When people whose opinion we value judge us to be selfish, that judgment can hurt our feelings, damage our selfesteem, and worst of all, make us question our motivation. Are we in fact being self-centered? Are we putting our own needs above the needs of others? Maybe we really are acting out of selfishness.

As I write this chapter, the news media have been reporting a string of incidents from around the country that suggest that serious civil rights violations are occurring. It's heartbreaking to read about the victimization of innocent people, and maybe I have a special sensitivity to these news stories because these cases are exactly like the ones I used to handle regularly. Last night, a close friend texted me a message that said, "Please come out of retirement, the country needs you." Well, that was a gross exaggeration to be sure. Everyone has the obligation to fight against injustice, but no single person can stop it. Nevertheless, I knew that as a practicing lawyer I could fight in a special way, and maybe a more effective way. Was I being selfish because I would not leave the classroom, reopen my law office, and jump back into the harness?

I firmly believe that the answer to that question is a clear "no." And let me emphasize here that these questions have nothing to do with being a lawyer rather than being anything else. Getting off the train, any train, is a big step, and some people will criticize you for it no matter what particular kind of train you're riding. Maybe your new income will be less than what you earned before. If so, aren't you being irresponsible to place your own "fun" above the needs of your family and dependents? Maybe your new life will be more pleasant than what you had before. If so, aren't you being lazy to leave a harder life for an easier one? Maybe your Personal Renaissance will not utilize the skills or talents that contributed to your earlier success. If so, aren't you being ungrateful for those skills and talents and wasting your abilities? For me, it was legal ability. For you, it could be anything. Are you a talented chef? An effective teacher? A compassionate nurse? A caring doctor? An accurate bookkeeper? A brave firefighter? An efficient salesperson? A skilled carpenter? A capable manager? A reliable employee? A terrific something else? If so, it's wonderful that you have developed skills that allow you to make an important contribution to your community. The world needs chefs, teachers, nurses, doctors, bookkeepers, firefighters, salespersons, carpenters, managers, employees, and yes, even lawyers. But that doesn't mean that the person who serves those needs has to be *you* or *me*. You have been responsible for your whole life, or else you wouldn't have arrived at the place you are today. You have done the right thing and taken care of the people who have relied on you. It's OK for you to take care of yourself now.

Let me repeat that:

It's OK for you to take care of yourself now.

Don't get me wrong. If you were going to give up a career as a kindergarten teacher to become a cocaine dealer, or if your First Blank aspiration was to become a bank robber, then I would be standing front and center shooting the arrows of criticism straight at you. But as we have already discussed, your Personal Renaissance will grow from what you love. Something was missing before, and now you are setting out to find it. A person who has lived a good and decent life of integrity will probably not wake up one day and feel an urgent desire to create a new life of squalor and depravity. Your Personal Renaissance, whatever it turns out to be, will give you the opportunity to do worthwhile things and to serve your fellow human beings. You will just be doing it in a different way.

I have a friend who was once a very successful manager at a large university. She handled the administrative details of major scientific research projects. Everything from applying for the financial grants that funded the research, to coordinating the work of the scientists, to editing the final reports—she did all of those things and more. The research could not have proceeded without her contributions. But one day she realized that she no longer wanted to do those things. She had gone to college and then to graduate school to prepare herself for the important work that she was doing, but that work was no longer rewarding. It no longer nurtured her spirit. The life that she had been living for so long had grown partial and inauthentic. It was time for her to drop the embroidery needle and find a paintbrush.

Sometimes the smallest detail about our condition will prepare us to create a Personal Renaissance, and in her case that small detail was her realization that her office didn't have any windows. She made a good salary, her work was important, and she was good at it. It was a nice enough office, and she must have always known that there were no windows there. But one day those windowless walls just seemed to speak to her. And do you know what they said?

CLACKETYCLACKETYCLACK!

She was riding somebody else's train. She found Emergency Stop, pulled the handle, and walked out of her carriage into a specialized school to learn massage therapy. Today she is a licensed massage therapist who looks forward to going to work every single day. She helps people feel better. She relieves pain and stress. And she has a window.

Is she irresponsible? Is she being lazy? Has she acted selfishly? Certainly not. Being a massage therapist is every bit as important as being a research manager. For that matter, being a research manager is every bit as important as being a massage therapist. Her new career, her Personal Renaissance, grew out of the dissatisfaction that told her she should be concentrating on personal energy and wellness instead of corporate energy and management. Sure, that was what was best for her. But her old job was important, too. What happened to all of that critical work and the people who had once depended on her to do a good job? Good question.

Guess what? The university did not have to shut its doors when she left. The president and board of trustees did not close down the science department or stop doing research. Somehow, the world that she left behind found a way to exist without her.

When my other friend sent me that text about the need for me to get back to work and stop civil rights violations, I didn't ignore her. I responded. "I did that job for decades," I replied. "I have passed the baton."

And so I have.

Former French president Charles de Gaulle once quipped that every graveyard is filled with indispensable men. Indeed. My old world has done just fine without me. So will yours. And anyway, I think I can make a difference and change the world for the better as a teacher and a writer. I do not believe for a minute that being a lawyer is any better or more indispensable than being a professor. Or a chef, teacher, nurse, doctor, book-keeper, firefighter, salesperson, carpenter, employee, research manager, or massage therapist. Or, for that matter, a mountain climber, beekeeper, navigator, poet, or rocket scientist.

You can dodge the arrows of the Know-It-Alls, the Settlers, and the Moralizers. There is, however, one arrow shooter we haven't discussed yet. He or she is the closest one of all, and maybe the most unexpected. Certainly the most dangerous.

Just look in the mirror.

TENTH GUIDEPOST

Your old world and you will both flourish independently.

CHAPTER 11

PANDORA'S JAR

"While I breathe, I hope."
CICERO

There may be one last thing holding you back. It's more than a little sensitive, maybe even insulting, but it has to be said: Maybe you don't feel that you deserve to live out your dreams. Maybe you don't feel you are good enough for a Personal Renaissance. Believe me, some people feel that way, and I don't know if you are one of them. Some people have been profoundly damaged by the lives they have lived so far. Their circumstances are peculiar to them, but the heartbreak is all too common. Maybe it has been poverty. Maybe cruel parents. Failed marriages. Childhood abuse. Ungrateful friends. A neglectful family. Physical challenges. Emotional distress. Illness. Sadness. Misery. No matter what a person's specific tragedies have been, they often leave that person with a pervasive and persistent sense that they are just not good enough. Not deserving of pleasure. Unworthy of joy.

So many things have defeated them that they have grown used to defeat. Their life history seems so uniformly dreadful that they accept every awful event that comes to them. They long ago stopped being surprised by deprivation and loss. The good life they may have envisioned for themselves once upon a time has been sliced away, amputated piece by piece, until all that's left of it is a raw and painful nub and the fading memories of what it once felt like to be hopeful and intact. No wonder that person can't anticipate the individual fulfillment of a Personal Renaissance. No wonder he or she can't brave the frontier outside the train. All the person knows is fear and danger. Being exposed to uncertainty and risk is too much to ask. It is nothing short of impossible—more than they believe they could ever do.

If this all sounds uncomfortably familiar, then you have to be careful of the deadliest arrow of all—the arrow of unworthiness. There is no way to dodge this one because you shoot it at yourself and you know the target by heart. The arrow is deadly and your aim is true. Instead of dodging it, you have to learn how to avoid shooting it in the first place.

If this sounds like you, believe me, you have lots of company.

And so did I, because that was once me, too.

I told you about the good life that I walked away from to find one that was even better, but I haven't yet told you too much about the life that came before *that*. It is, to be completely honest about it, a memory that is painful for me to dredge up, but I know that some people reading this book will ignore whatever assurances I give that they can do what I've done. They may still have a Third Blank mentality—"You could do it because you're special. You're so much more _____ than I am." Or maybe someone is stuck at The Second Blank: "I could never do that because I am _____." Maybe they are thinking that they are different and special because they are especially unworthy. They may see themselves as doomed to fail. Preordained to incompleteness. My story proves that both of those ways of thinking are wrong.

Here it is.

I was born to an immigrant family in one of the last remaining industrial cities in Connecticut. The surrounding hamlets and villages were straight out of a Currier and Ives catalog of New England loveliness, but my town was dingy and hard. It was a city of factories, broken sidewalks, and smoke. My father had immigrated to America when he was a boy, all alone and without contacts or resources. He had struggled to make a living as a dishwasher and cook and eventually married my mother in what was almost certainly an arranged marriage. By the time I was old enough to understand all the details, they had become confused in the swirling mists of family mythology. The things I did know for sure, however, were that neither of my parents had ever finished grade school, let alone high school or college, and that we were poor. I had two much older brothers, and I never discovered or understood how I came to be born ten and twenty years after them.

My father eventually became a talented chef, but without opportunities and connections he was forced to make do as a short-order cook. When I was born he was working in a little diner on a dirty backstreet, right behind the post office and next to a municipal parking lot. Sometimes my mother and I would ride the bus to the diner and sit patiently until my father could take a moment away from the hamburgers and scrambled eggs. He would come out of the kitchen in his white shirt and apron with a little tin cup of vanilla ice cream for me. I can remember that the ice cream made the outside of the cup get all frosty and cold. I later learned that he had tried and failed in business—restaurants and grocery stores mostly—and that this humble job was all that kept our family from starvation. No one could have been happy about the unexpected arrival of another mouth to feed—but there I was. The third son in a family that was barely surviving and that was, in any event, still in the process of recovering from tragedy.

You see, shortly before my birth my oldest brother had started attending a local state college. It was one of the schools that in those days was called a "teachers' college," because that's what you could do with the degree you earned there. My brother, though, had different aspirations. He wanted to be an electrical engineer, so he took whatever science and math courses were offered close to home and hoped that he could someday transfer to the University of Connecticut to finish his degree. My parents must have scrimped and saved for years, decades probably, to put together the little bit of money that would get him started before the hopedfor scholarships kicked in. For a while it must have seemed as if the American Dream that my father had chased across the ocean might actually come true. But then it didn't.

As he attended college, my brother started getting sick. And then sicker, and then sicker still. Eventually he learned that he had a disease that was killing his kidneys and would surely kill him, too. There was no cure, and all my parents could do was sit by his hospital bed and watch his body become more and more bloated with the fluids that his failing kidneys could not eliminate. They watched him drowning inside his own skin and getting closer and closer to the grave.

Eventually, in an almost unreal stroke of good luck, my parents located a doctor who was experimenting with a new and untested treatment for that disease. He agreed to take my brother's case, the treatment worked, and my brother was cured. The family had been through a year and more of hell. Every dime of savings had been spent on medical bills, and so a return to college for my brother was out of the question. The poverty that had once been manageable and merely crippling was now overwhelming. It was all our parents could do to keep a roof above us.

And then it seemed as if they would not be able to do even that. The meager apartment in which we lived, a second-floor walk-up in a neighborhood filled with ethnic grocers and discount stores, was owned by another Greek immigrant—but he had money and property. One Sunday afternoon he drove over to our home in his shiny Cadillac and told my father that he was going to give our apartment to his nephew who had just arrived in America. We had to leave. Just like that. There could be no argument. He was commanding, not requesting, and all my father could do was listen without speaking a word. When the landlord left, my family huddled around a window and watched him drive away as my mother cried that we would soon be homeless. "He'll throw us all into the street," she screamed, and then she screamed it again and again until my father told her to be quiet because she was scaring me. He was right. That image—the window, the screams, the shiny car, the atmospheric terror, the panicky helplessness, and my father's impotence in the face of the powerful landlord—is the very first thing I can remember. For me, that memory is how life and childhood began.

The next place we lived was a tiny apartment on the ground floor of a small house owned by another Greek family. The apartment had two bedrooms for the five of us. My middle brother and I shared a room, and my oldest brother, the one who had been sick, slept on a foldout sofa bed in the front room. The bedroom I shared was so small that with two twin beds there was no room for any other furniture. There was a small closet, but to fit both beds we had to block the door shut, so it was of no use to us. I remember that there were hooks on the back of the bedroom door to hang some of our clothes, and the rest had to be kept in the basement. The painted plaster walls were stained and cracked, and some rooms, my bedroom among them, had big holes that exposed the lath boards under the plaster. I started school in that apartment, but not before the greatest catastrophe of all.

It was the summer that I was five years old; I would be starting kindergarten in the fall. I remember that the kitchen was the largest room in that tiny apartment. To my childish perspective it seemed huge, but I'm sure it really wasn't very big at all. I jumped out of bed on the third Sunday morning that August and started to walk down the short, dark hallway from my bedroom to the kitchen. I noticed that the apartment was quiet. I couldn't hear my father's heavily Greek-accented morning voice, or my brothers or my mother. Strange. My mother was probably in the kitchen, and maybe everyone else was in there, too. But why weren't they talking?

When I stopped at the kitchen door, I saw my mother sitting at the table. The sink was behind her. There were white-washed cabinets to her right, my left. One of them was open and there were a few glasses missing from the shelf. The floor was covered with cheap, sparkly linoleum. I can still summon up a vision of that scene as if I were watching it right now in highdefinition video. Her sister Mary was sitting with her. Both women were bent over the table with their heads hanging low. No one else was in there, and they didn't notice me at first. I had never seen my Aunt Mary in our home before. She and my mother had been waging some kind of trivial but all-consuming sisterly feud for all of my young life, and although I had no idea what their disagreement was about (and still don't), I knew that it wielded a fearsome power. Mary was not allowed in our apartment, and only the direst catastrophe could have made my mother open our doors to her. When the sisters saw me standing small and bewildered in the doorway, they stared at each other for a moment too long. It made me worry even more, and I remember starting to shake a little. My mother, heavyset and bathrobed, stood up slowly and said, "I guess I have to tell him." And then she did.

My father had died the night before. He had gone to a nearby restaurant and met some friends for dinner, newly arrived Greek immigrants who were in town for the weekend. After dinner he walked up the hill that led to our house, came into the apartment, and collapsed with a heart attack. My brothers were at the funeral home with his body when I woke up on that August Sunday, and my mother had called her sister for moral support. She told me with an inarticulate and dreadful directness that I was fatherless: "Your father has gone away and he won't ever come back because he's dead." Then she left me alone in the front room to cry with a child's feeble and unsuccessful attempt at grief and understanding. Whatever I was supposed to do to confront that cataclysm was something I had to work out by myself. Someone could have tried to comfort me, I suppose, but they were busy with their own problems and didn't. If all of that sounds sad and dreadful, believe me, it was only the beginning. After that day, things went from bad to awful.

After my father's death, my mother sank into a despondent lunacy from which she never escaped. She hated the life that fate had given her, and that hatred made her despise everyone who inhabited that life. She became cruel and abusive, and like all hateful bullies she saved the worst treatment for whomever was too weak to defend themselves—and that was usually me. From the Sunday morning that I sat in that front room wondering what "because he's dead" meant through the many years until I left home, I lived in a toxic stew of cruelty and unhappiness. I won't get into the details, but they're not pretty.

If I sound as if I am wallowing in self-pity and looking for sympathy, I'm really not. I appreciate the good fortune that gave me many advantages: I have been healthy, I am intelligent, and I have a lot of people in my world who care about me deeply. Eventually, I used my circumstances to learn how to stand up for myself, and then I made it my mission to stand up for others: people who were themselves too weak and helpless to survive their troubles without help. Maybe that mission is why I stayed on the lawyer train for so long.

I am telling you this story because I want you to understand—and believe—that you can resolve to create a Personal Renaissance from any starting point at all. You may have landed in a terrible place. Poverty, helplessness, deprivation, losses, abuse, lovelessness, and neglect. Maybe other calamities befell you. Newsflash: You didn't deserve it.

Listen carefully: *You did not deserve it.*

You have *always* deserved something better than what life gave you, and the fact that you didn't get it was unfair. It was wrong. It was cruel. Today, right now, you deserve a better life. Maybe you have suffered so much that you have convinced yourself that you cannot possibly stop suffering. Maybe you feel—as I once did—that not even the strongest, smartest, toughest person in the world could overcome the constellation of misery and misfortune you have faced. I'm here to tell you that those feelings are wrong. The sense of learned helplessness that comes from being helpless for so long, the sense of defeatism that comes from having been defeated so thoroughly, that false reality is just another train that we have to get off.

Thousands of years ago, a poet named Hesiod told a story about a woman named Pandora. Pandora was created by the gods of Olympus and they gave her every gift—life and beauty and health and more. In fact, the name "Pandora" means exactly that—"every gift." Pandora was the first human woman, and she was destined to give birth to a new race, a new age. But Zeus, the king of Olympus, decided that humanity did not deserve such happiness, so he gave Pandora a jar filled with demons who carried every kind of trouble, pain, and agony. When Pandora opened the jar one day, they all flew out. They have been flying around the world causing human woe and suffering ever since.

But one of the other Olympians saw what Zeus was up to and took pity on humanity. He managed to sneak something else into Pandora's jar. It was a little jewel, a gemstone that was too heavy to fly away and something that Pandora could find and hold on to for the life of all mankind. It was the jewel of Hope. According to Hesiod, that final gift was enough to allow men and women, Pandora's every child, to survive every misery that escaped from her jar.

I know—it's just a story. But maybe, like me, you can recognize the feeling that the universe—Zeus, fate, karma, destiny, genetics, history, whatever—has filled your jar of life with wretchedness and not much else. I have discovered—now, eventually, later in my life, *finally*—that that feeling is false. I agree with the Danish philosopher Søren Kierkegaard, who once said, "Hope is the passion for that which is possible." You may not have always thought that happiness was possible for you; you may have started reading this book thinking that a Personal Renaissance was beyond your reach.

It isn't.

Pandora gave birth to a hopeful race in spite of the demons in her jar. And you? You can rebirth your life from resolve to Renaissance. I did.

Believe me, that possibility is the greatest gift of all.

ELEVENTH GUIDEPOST

You can't bury your past—but you can prevent it from burying you.

PART FOUR

Essence

"That dominant individualism...
withal that buoyancy and exuberance
which comes with freedom,
these are traits of the Frontier...."
FREDERICK JACKSON TURNER

INTRODUCTION

Frederick Jackson Turner's notion of a constantly moving boundary that divides the old and the new remains a powerful metaphor for the magnetic pull of opportunity and resolve. But when he gave his speech in 1893, there was a big problem with the frontier: it was gone. Three years earlier the government had announced that the whole country had been populated; there was no more unsettled land in America. "And now, four centuries from the discovery of America, at the end of a hundred years of life under the Constitution, the frontier has gone, and with its going has closed the first period of American history." If the wilderness beyond the frontier really did make America, what would happen now that there was none of it left? Would the spirit of initiative and self-determination disappear with it?

Obviously not. When the geographical frontier closed, frontiers of the imagination opened up to take its place. Forty-five years after Turner's speech, President Franklin Roosevelt encouraged Americans to conquer the frontier of "insecurity, of human want and fear." Then came Kennedy's "New Frontier" speech in

1960. Then astronaut Buzz Aldrin came home from the moon and called space travel "the next frontier in the human experience." Astronomer Edwin Hubble knew that science allowed humanity to explore "the frontier of the known universe." Turner himself knew that frontier crossings would morph from the geography of the land to the geography of the human spirit. "He would be a rash prophet who should assert that the expansive character of American life has now entirely ceased. Movement has been its dominant fact, and, unless this training has no effect upon a people, the American energy will continually demand a wider field for its exercise."

Edmund Hillary surmounted the frontier of audacity. Siddhartha crossed the frontier of understanding. Grandma Moses crossed the frontier of creativity. The Curiosity rover crossed the frontier of determination.

Even the inventor of the frontier thesis itself, Frederick Jackson Turner, crossed his own personal frontier on that summer day in Chicago when he pushed the boundary of conventional wisdom and changed the way historians and scholars understood the creation of America.

And as for you, your own Renaissance life waits for you—just across your own moving frontier of individual fulfillment.

CHAPTER 12

SPRINGTIME IN PARIS

*"Nature does not hurry,
yet everything is accomplished."*

LAO TZU

I eventually did finish graduate school and became a professor. Did that mean that I had reached my Personal Renaissance? How could I know—how can any of us truly know—when we've conquered our Life's Frontier? What will life feel like once it has been rebirthed?

These are important questions, so now let's talk about results.

It's time for another thought experiment.

This time, imagine that you and a friend are having a special night out. It's your birthday, so you have come to the fanciest, most expensive, and most popular French restaurant in town. You had to make reservations three weeks ago, and the prices are more than you would usually feel comfortable spending. But what the heck? It's your birthday, so you're pulling out the stops.

As soon as you enter the place, you can see what all the buzz is about. The dining room is gorgeous. Opulent but tasteful. Simple but luxurious. The maître d' seats you at a terrific table and gives you menus to look at while you wait for your server. Every available square inch of the room is packed with customer seating, and every table is full. No wonder you had to call so far in advance. While you wait for your server, you look around the dining room. You can see some of the plated dinners and they look amazing, but what really draws your attention is the professionalism of the staff. After a moment, your gaze lands on one waiter in particular as he confidently weaves his way through the narrow aisles.

You can't take your eyes off of him. He carries dinner plates in both hands; sometimes he balances a heavy tray on his shoulder. He delivers the food smoothly and efficiently. He strolls rapidly but never rushes. He politely introduces each patron's meal, and he can knowledgeably answer any question. He has the economy of motion of a dancer, precise in every step and movement. What really holds your attention, though, are the ways that he makes it all seem so easy. Effortless. He speedwalks through the crowd, glancing ahead to the next spot he will occupy. He times his arrival at the kitchen door to catch it on the backswing, and he spins and twirls to pass his colleagues in the narrow spaces. His face wears the calm smile that comes from the confidence that his skill allows. You are impressed. It's fun to watch an expert ply his craft.

But then you see another waiter. He has none of the zest nor the effortless grace of the first one. It isn't as though he is a klutz or a slob. In fact, he seems to be, in his own way, equally efficient. He delivers the food flawlessly, he is cordial and polite, but he wears a face of bland disinterest. His moves are workmanlike, but they are somehow too deliberate. The way he carries himself is excessively formal, forced, and strained. Rigid and stiff. Instead of waltzing around the dining room like a dancer, he marches through it like a storm trooper. He seems to have studied the other waiter and tries hard to imitate him. Indeed, he is trying too hard. He has learned the mechanics of the job, but he doesn't even come close to making it look natural.

The Great Waiter has a smooth elegance that comes from his core. The Bad Waiter does not. Compared to the lithe virtuoso whom he mimics, the second guy is a robot. An automaton. The Great Waiter possesses the essence of professional grace and precision, while the other waiter is simply playing the role. His existence is a pretense, an impostor to authenticity.

This story of the two waiters is based, loosely, on the work of the French writer Jean-Paul Sartre. During the twentieth-century heyday of European intellectualism, he lived and worked on Paris's Left Bank. He earned and refused the Nobel Prize in literature because he didn't think that a writer should "allow himself to be turned into an institution." He was best known for his work on a theory that helped introduce a new way of thinking about human development: *Existentialism*. That is why he and his waiters are important to us.

Before Sartre and the other existentialists, many philosophers believed in something called *essentialism*. That idea went all the way back to Socrates, maybe even further, and it taught that everything in the world has some set of core qualities that define it. Those qualities are called its *essence*. A table has the essence of table-ness, and a boat has the essence of boat-ness. That is how we know which is which. If tables and boats had the same essential qualities—four legs and a surface, for example—there would be no way to tell them apart. Naturally, the essence of every object comes before the actual existence of the object itself. Before a carpenter can build a table, he has to know about the essence of table-ness so that he can set out to build a thing that expresses that essence. In other words, a thing's essence must precede its existence.

Hard-core essentialists applied that belief to everything, even to human beings. They believed that there had to be an essential human nature that preceded and predestined the existence of human beings in general and of any individual man or woman in particular. The human race as a whole may be predestined to be rational or irrational, selfish or generous, smart or stupid, but whatever traits form part of our essence, we are stuck with them. The qualities of your humanness were written into your destiny long before you were born, long before you ever existed. And so were your limitations.

The theory of human essentialism goes beyond the nuts and bolts of physical and psychological characteristics. Not only is there an overriding essence for the nature of humanity, but there are smaller, more specific essences that define every variety of individual human life. Teachers have an essence. Students have an essence. Lawyers, doctors, builders, artists, cashiers, typists, all the way down the line. Everyone is acting out the role that their particular slice of human nature has written for them. We are all actors on a cosmic stage, waiters in the universal café. We play at being free, but we actually just express the nature of our preexistence.

If this sounds pretty bleak, that's because it is. And it gets even worse. What if you are predestined to be a hot-tempered, lazy, beer-guzzling couch potato? How do you escape that dreary fate? Sorry. You don't. Put your feet up, grab a six-pack, and scream at the television. Welcome to essentialism.

Sartre would have nothing of that. His brand of philosophy turned essentialism on its head and denied that anything, or anyone, has a primordial nature that governs or limits its potential. In fact, Sartre became famous for expressing his ideas in a pithy slogan—*existence precedes essence*. To understand what he meant, let's go back to the French restaurant and take another look at those two waiters.

In an existentialist universe, and therefore in the French restaurant of Sartre's thought experiment, every man and woman is responsible for creating his or her own life. We create our individual situation. We actually manufacture our own essence. We do those things by deciding how we are going to act, to think, to behave. We decide for ourselves how we are going to exist, and the existence that we create for ourselves determines the essence of our individual human natures. Our existence, the existence that we create for ourselves, comes first. Our essential nature comes later, sometimes much later. Renaissance can't be rushed. Existence precedes essence.

The two waiters prove that point. The first one—smooth, competent, effortless, and natural—wasn't born that way. He was not predestined to be a great waiter. He animated his career with vitality. He invested his life with resolve, and he became a great waiter because he committed his very existence to that resolve. That commitment, that investment, that existential investment, created the essence of great-waiter-ness that you admired while he danced around the dining room with his dinner plates and trays. Bad Waiter—stiff, forced, and unnatural—never made that commitment. He may be able to put food on your table, but he could never put his heart on the line. He never dedicated his existence to create an essence of greatness. You knew that as soon as you saw him.

But so what? Maybe Bad Waiter never had the same breaks as Great Waiter. Maybe he doesn't have the natural gifts that it takes to be great—the strength, the verve, the personality. Maybe he doesn't want to be great. The resolve to greatness is not important to him. He's satisfied with his mediocrity. What's wrong with that?

According to Sartre, there is plenty wrong with that, and I agree. First of all, if he can't resolve to be a great waiter, then he should resolve to be a great something else or at least an authentic something else, because right now he is wasting his existence. No one is trapped in a role that they don't want to play; no one is condemned to be mediocre. In fact, and here is Sartre's second most famous quote, everyone on Earth is *condemned to be free.* Everyone is *free* to manufacture the end product of their own essence out of the raw material of their existence. But there's more to it than that. Not only are you free to create your own life, you are *required* to. You have to. You don't have any choice in the matter. You are creating your life, your essence, with every decision you make and every action you take, whether you like it or not. Bad Waiter may grumble and grouse and wonder why he gets such rotten tips, but he has created the very life that disappoints him. No one and no thing put him there or keeps him there. Sartre says that Bad Waiter's problem is that he is treating his world with *bad faith*: with an unfair, self-defeating, delusional artificiality. His existence has created his essence, and if he doesn't like the one he's got, then he needs to create a better one. After all, he is condemned to be free.

Around the corner from Paris's Hotel Andre there is a small café that, so far as I can recall, has no name. I discovered it around 2 a.m. as I explored the Latin Quarter, very near where Jean-Paul Sartre died on April 15, 1980. Thirty-three years to the day after his death, I had flown here to deliver a speech at an academic conference at the University of Versailles. The café without a name was about the size of my living room at home. The waiter led me by my elbow with one hand and carried a silver-dollar sized table over his head with the other. We walked through the mob to find a couple of square inches of empty floor space. He dropped the table and grabbed me a nearby chair. He screamed "Que voulez-vous?" ("What would you like?") as he leaned close enough that my ear knocked the loose ash off his cigarette. I ordered a Desperado Longneck and sat down. The place was packed and chaotic. There was a tiny stage about two feet from my table with a female vocalist and a guy playing the piano. She was wearing an electric-blue sequined formal. He seemed to be wearing the same suit that he had slept in for the last week and a half. They were performing American torch songs. I came in on "Smoke Gets in Your Eyes" and stayed until first light. I drank Desperados while their repertoire cycled around two or three times and had a *croque monsieur* for breakfast. It was springtime in Paris, the springtime of my Personal Renaissance.

My friend Katy has been reading some of these chapters as I finish them. After the previous chapter, Katy wrote to me with her comments and then asked me an important question. "Maybe I'm at my Personal Renaissance. I think really I could be. How can I know?"

Katy was as much of a Personal Renaissance candidate as anyone I knew. She had once spent many years riding the business train, leading a massive corporate organization before she pulled her Emergency Stop a few years ago. She decompressed a little and then decided to take a part-time job managing a small boutique. It would be a new experience, a world apart from the corporation she once managed. It would give her something to do — get her out in the community and meet new people — and it could be fun. For a while it was, but then Katy saw the "part-time" hours expand until they filled up all her days. She opened the store and closed it, she took work home, and (of course) the owner was happy to save on payroll and let Katy do all the work. Before too long, Katy realized that she had not really gotten off the Do-Too-Much-for-Others-at-the-Expense-of-Your-Own-Wellness Train but had simply moved to a different car, transferring her soul-bleaching corporate ways to the boutique world. So she pulled Emergency Stop once again, a little harder this time, jumped out of her carriage, and started walking the uncertain path toward her own essence.

But now that she was on the path to Personal Renaissance, she had asked the best question of all: How do we know when we get there? There are no navigational buoys to mark our arrival. We won't find a "Welcome to Renaissance" road sign.

Or will we? One of my most persistent complaints about being a lawyer was that I was *always* worrying about my clients and their problems. After all, many of them were at risk of losing their lives or futures, and the only thing that stood between them and their destruction was me. If you were the client, wouldn't you want your lawyer to worry himself sick about you all the time? I would. So that's what I did for them.

I worried all day long. I woke up at night thinking about new ways to save them. I agonized over their troubles 24/7/365. I was never out of the office, because I carried the office around in my frontal lobes and I never stopped thinking about the lives I was sworn to defend.

It was honorable and crucial work, no question about it, and in the long run I did save most of them. But one day, after I saw Emergency Stop but before I pulled the handle, I asked a friend a question that was sort of like Katy's question to me: "What's next?" If I stopped practicing law and no longer had clients to agonize over, what would come next for that 24/7/365 stew of concentration, problem-solving, creativity, and worry? My son the cognitive scientist is an expert on the workings of the human brain, and he talks about the brain as if it is a city, every part of it made up of "cognitive real estate." I used that concept to frame my question: What would I build on the cognitive real estate that would no longer have the Client Crisis Hotel on it? I didn't know. Maybe I would build the New Problem Condominiums there. Maybe I would just carry my own soul-bleaching tendencies to another carriage on my train and spend all my time worrying about new and different things. My health? The state of the world? Nanite invasions? Asteroid impacts? Was I just an overactive worrier, destined to suffer anguish no matter what my circumstances? Was that the nature of my pre-existential essence? Was I condemned to be not free?

I refused to believe that, and I was proven right. When I got off *The Imaginary Train* of my pre-essence, I discovered that the cognitive real estate that had once supported an overpopulated community of anguish and distress was now occupied by, well, it took me a while to identify it, but I eventually recognized it as *tranquility*. I was at peace. My thinking was less frantic and more ordered. I smiled more. My friends noticed it. My kids noticed it. People who hadn't seen me in years thought that maybe I had suffered a nervous breakdown and was medicated. No. No medication. Just quiescence. Calm. Composure.

Wow.

You see, when you live an inauthentic life, it takes a lot of your emotional resources to maintain the consciousness that is not genuinely yours. You are always erecting ramparts against inauthenticity. You are constantly fighting a holding action against psychic marauders like fear, misery, sadness, and discontent. You greet each morning and every nighttime with the perfect knowledge that the wrongness of your essence is eroding your spirit. It's a hard way to live.

How do you know that you have created *your* Personal Renaissance? The best sign of your arrival is this: the life that once was so hard to live now becomes *easy*. Well, maybe not completely easy but *easier*. You may still have money troubles, your dog may still pee on the rug, and those ten extra pounds are not just going to evaporate. But you will look in the morning mirror and no longer see the sour-faced Bad Waiter looking back at you. You will be more often happy than sad. You will be kinder and more gracious, and less angry. You will feel yourself dancing through the French restaurant of your life, instead of goose-stepping from one table to the next, grumbling at the customers. This recognition may come upon you as a gradual progression from obscurity to clarity. It may hit you in a dizzying moment of vertiginous free fall, or it may tap you on the shoulder during the third playing of "As Time Goes By" in the darkest café in Paris. No matter. All of the personal energy that once went to anguish, bitterness, and woe will now be available to you for however else you choose to spend it.

TWELFTH GUIDEPOST

Your personal Renaissance culminates with your recognition of your true essence.

The Imaginary Train

It's been a long time since you got off the train. You have traveled far and wide and seen many fantastic sights. You have learned much about the world and about yourself. Each day has been a thrilling voyage through essentiality—equal parts risk and wonder, equal parts gamble and adventure. One day, you are wandering toward tomorrow when you hear the faintest sound of a distant clackety-clack. Some train, somewhere, is rolling down its tracks.

You can't see anything yet, and you have walked so far and so aimlessly since you left your railroad car that you don't know if it's your old track or another one. You hadn't considered that there might be other tracks with other trains and other riders looking and wondering about other Emergency Stop switches. It makes perfect sense, though. Why should yours be the only one?

You keep walking in the direction of the sound, and finally you come upon a set of tracks. You can see that a train is speeding toward you from a faraway point just below the horizon. The roar of the engine and the clacketyclack of the wheels as *they pass over each rail joint grow louder and louder as the train draws near. It passes the point where you are standing, roaring with a blast of air and noise that almost knocks you over. Then, within a second, while you are still pushing back against the wind to hold your balance, you hear it. It is sudden and huge, and the first thought that goes through your mind is "so that's what it sounded like from the outside."*

SCREE-EEE-EECH.

The wheels slide and skid against the steel rail as they lock in place, struggling for traction. Smoke rises from the tracks and from under the carriage as the air brake pistons fight the onslaught of velocity and momentum. You stand there wide-eyed and amazed as the roaring motor slows and slows and stops, its mighty stampede quelled by someone's hand upon the switch. But whose?

A Discovery on a Coastal Road

"All men dream: but not equally.
Those who dream by night in the dusty recesses
of their minds wake in the day to find that
it was vanity: but the dreamers of the day are
dangerous men, for they may act their dreams
with open eyes, to make it possible."

T. E. Lawrence

This December in Athens was colder than the last one, but in spite of the chill, the restaurants and cafés all along Adrianou Street set their tables outside, next to the walking path that separated them from the ancient ruins of the Agora. The Green Line metro train rumbled past from time to time. It was Athens's first route. Line 1. Its cars were grimy, graffitied, and old, but compared to the floodlighted Acropolis that ruled the skyline from high above, everything else was new. Even the Green Line.

All of the eating places had waiters who served as ropers, hawking the menus and promising authentic Greek food. Well, it was Athens, after all.

"Yes, Mister. Good evening. Would you like dinner?" "Yassou, what do you like to eat?" "Moussaka? Octopus? Toast?"

It didn't matter if the pitch was obvious or non sequitur. Every tourist had to eat sometime, and they were all willing to pay a premium for tables with clear sightlines to the Parthenon. They all wanted "real" Greek food so that they could go home and gossip expertly at the country club or the supermarket about how the pastitsio at Gus's local diner had too much nutmeg. "But you should have tasted the stuff we had at that little spot in Athens. It was simply *perfect*!"

Locals hustled down the walking path with their shopping bags and their smartphones. Office workers headed home or to their barstools and their ouzo. Lovers strolled more slowly and hugged away the cold. Potential lovers choreographed that age-old dance of smiles, jokes, and whispers that would propel them from desire to uncertainty. Teenagers stopped from time to time for selfies with the ruins. Long ago, the maiden Athena had won the name and soul of the city. In eight days, Christian churches around the world would be celebrating another virgin miracle. It was the season when wonderful things could happen.

A hundred tavernas all served the same authentic Greek menu, but everyone claimed a favorite. The Kouzina Acropoli was my favorite tonight. The roper had seated me at the front of the terrace under a gas-flamed heater and cranked it up to full blast. My table, four feet from the flame and 100 yards from the trial of Socrates, was almost too warm. My nearness to the walkway made me a prime prospect for every preteen entrepreneur peddling roses, trinkets, and toys. Women of every age strolled past, protected from bother by the rough-hewn but explicit code of Greek manners that outlawed any harassment.

I finished my lamb shank, red wine, and honeyed cake and then strolled up Irakleidon Street to the Parthenon Bar. Giorgio the bartender gave me his standard faux-grave look and a bottle of Mythos. Afterward, we would share shots of raki—"I like it because it's like ouzo," Giorgio once explained, "only stronger." Fortunately, my sublet was only two blocks away or that first night would have seen me sleeping on the boulevard.

As I sat down at the bar, Giorgio was in the middle of cooking up some fancy drink concoction in a long-handled pot over a gas burner. A few liqueurs and cinnamon and some-thing else and a tincture of something red. He funneled it from the pot into a tall thin bottle that went to another customer, but he held back a shot glass–full for me. "Take this, my friend." It tasted like wildfire mixed with honey. I had another one and then another Mythos.

Giorgio and I made the usual jokes about how little Greek I spoke and how strange I was to be always writing things in my notebook. He took a break from our conversation to walk over to the end of the bar and flirt with the gorgeous twen-ty-something who was drawing his portrait on a napkin with her lipstick. His T-shirt had a silkscreened picture of a ram with very long, curly horns. It looked to be as old and dirty as the Green Line metro.

It was 1 a.m. in Athens, and I was part of the life of the city. Five thousand miles from home.

Giorgio's friend Evangelos came in and sat down beside me. I had met him last week. He was an engineer and longed to move to America. We spoke about his work and my visit and the city and the raki. Tonight I told him that I wanted to spend a few days on an island before I went home. I had planned to sail to the island of Naxos, but that was five hours away by the fastest boat. I asked Evangelos for alternatives.

"Aegina," he said, and his face lit up. "Close. Beautiful. Forty-five minutes. And the home of Kazantzakis. You know, Nikos Kazantzakis? Nikos the writer?"

Yes, I knew of Nikos the writer. Nikos Kazantzakis was one of the outstanding literary figures of the twentieth century. He had been nominated for the Nobel Prize nine times and created the wonderful character of Alexis Zorba— Zorba the Greek. His books were read by millions, and his fame spanned the globe. I knew that he was buried on the island of Rhodes beneath a gravestone that bore the epitaph, "I hope for nothing, I fear nothing, I am free." A great and fascinating man, and if there was a Kazantzakis homestead on Aegina, forty-five minutes away from my barstool, then I was going to see it. Of course.

So the next Tuesday found me at the port of Piraeus with a round-trip ticket to Aegina City. I had some clothes, my laptop, books, notebooks, and pens in a backpack that I bought the day before from an Athenian street vendor, and I boarded the *Flying Dolphin* hydrofoil. The boat looked a lot like a floating bus, but when it engaged its foil and skimmed across the surface of the Saronic Gulf, it jetted along at over thirty knots.

The port of Aegina was tiny, and its one and only street was lined with tavernas and cafés and kiosks selling pistachios. I had a reservation at the Regal Hotel and walked there in the warm sun. The manager was standing out front under his canopy, awaiting my arrival on the Dolphin. He introduced himself as Stavros. He was exactly my age and seemed to know everything about the gorgeous little island. In the course of the next three days I would learn his life story, his son's life story, their family history, and be invited to his cousin's wedding. I declined the wedding invitation, but by the time I returned to Athens we had become friends. When I checked out, he gave me a bag full of wild thyme that he had picked on a rocky hillside—"You must know the secret places where to look for the plant"—and he told me about the healing qualities of the herbs that made Hippocrates's reputation as the Father of Medicine. The Regal was a small hotel, just eight rooms, but the service was as friendly and caring as I would have received anywhere in the world. Evangelos had been right; Aegina was a wonderful place.

The next day I decided to find Nikos Kazantzakis's house. I asked Stavros for directions, and he took me outside his front door to the street, which I noticed for the first time was actually called Kazantzakis Avenue. He pointed up the road to the right and said, "Very easy. One and half kilometers. Straight ahead." So I thanked him, slung my camera over my shoulder, and headed north on the shore road that circumnavigated the island. One and a half kilometers? A three-kilometer round-trip? No problem.

Well, about ninety minutes later, I had climbed over an ancient temple to Apollo the Sun God, discovered a museum of local antiquity, and walked about six kilometers according to my smartphone's fitness app. Four times Stavros's estimate and no Kazantzakis house in sight. I had stopped for directions three times. I didn't have fluent Greek but I knew enough to say, "Pou eina to Spiti Kazantzaki," with an inquisitive inflection and a raised eyebrow. My accent was good enough that I was usually understood to be asking, "Where is the Kazantzakis House?" (I was), and everyone I asked pointed up the road with a waving, outstretched hand that told me to keep on walking.

Eight kilometers later still no Kazantzakis house. At one bend in the road, I saw a sign that pointed inland to a group of sun-bleached buildings in a sandy curtilage and identified them as the Kapralos Museum. I walked through the gate and found a young woman tending a garden. All I wanted from her were directions (again), but when she saw me pass through her gate she smiled warmly and asked me if I was there to see the art. "Of course," I said.

The museum consisted of six buildings; some were exposition spaces and the others were working studios, all dedicated to the twentieth-century artist and sculptor Christos Kapralos. I had never heard of Kapralos before that moment, but I quickly discovered that his work was magnificent. Huge abstract figures carved from eucalyptus tree trunks, marble blocks, and slabs of sandstone. Human shapes and skyward vectors. In front of the museum's entrance was an eleven-foot-tall bronze representation of a female villager, one of several works that he devoted to his own mother and to Greek motherhood in general. He had created murals of military battles from the Greek resistance and paintings of mythological events. I learned that the Aegina museum was one of six locations around Greece devoted to his work. His art was renowned throughout Europe and appeared in museums, galleries, and even in the Greek Parliament Building on Athens's Syntagma Square. By the time he died in 1993 at the age of eighty-four, he was one of Europe's most important artists.

The young woman who had invited me into the museum was a fount of information about the artist, and since that day I have learned a lot more about Kapralos on my own. I have studied every image of his work that I can find in books and online, and I have researched his art and his life. I have learned about his artwork, his ideals, and his dreams. He was a natural prodigy as a young child born into a poor, rural family. He fought in World War II and then returned home to the remote village of his birth and started his first studio. It was nothing more than a mud hut that he and his brother built, but he called it his "art laboratory." He believed passionately in freedom, tradition, and homeland. He achieved national fame and admiration and eventually represented Greece in a great international art festival. With the money he earned there, he reified the thing that he loved and built a beautiful studio on a sparkling Aegean island—a place where he could spend the rest of his life transforming the imaginings of his mind into real-life creations. The place he built was the realization of a lifetime of ambition and longing. It was the fulfillment of his Personal Renaissance. And there I was, smack dab in the middle of it. By accident.

After I thanked the museum curator, I continued walking up the shore road and eventually found the Kazantzakis home, but what I remember most clearly about that morning (aside from Stavros's lousy directions) is my discovery of a great artist and my good fortune to share, even briefly, in the space where he had made his dreams come true.

How did that discovery happen? It happened because I accepted my friend Jim's challenge, flew to Athens, followed a stranger's tip, sailed through unknown waters, reached an obscure new land, set out on an uncertain journey on foot, and embraced the serendipitous possibilities that accompany the act of getting hopelessly lost on a coastal road. That

December day on Aegina I came face-to-face with Renaissance. Of course.

And that was not the only strange and wonderful thing that happened that day.

THIRTEENTH GUIDEPOST

To find your Life's Frontier,
you may have to get lost first.

The Imaginary Train

As the smoke clears, you can see the outline of a door opening, and then, more clearly, you see someone walking down the steps. She is hesitant and walks with a halting gait, just like you did. She looks all around, gazing in every direction, stepping in one direction and then another, feeling the ground under her feet and the tall grass against her ankles. Just like you did. She turns around and looks at the track and is surprised to see that the train is gone. You are surprised, too. Neither of you saw or heard it leave. But like your train, this one had stayed long enough to finish its task of bringing her to this place. The place past and passed the other places where she didn't pull the switch.

She finally sees you standing there and she smiles. At first you know nothing about her, but then you know that you understand everything you need to. A moment ago she was rushing through her lifespan on someone else's schedule and in someone else's direction. She had ignored the handle of that Emergency Stop switch for a long time and was held off by the "Danger! Don't Touch!" sign. She was afraid of the future that *awaited her if she got off the train. She feared that she might get lost, or trip over a rock or a fallen branch or a hole in the ground, or get hurt. She had been afraid that the world outside the train could be rainy or cold. She knew that she might get sick, and that the outside world would be nothing like her train car. She was afraid of all of those things. Just like you were. Until finally—a mere moment ago—she wasn't afraid anymore.*

CHAPTER 14

How My Favorite Restaurant Got Its Name

"Thanks to impermanence,
everything is possible."
THICH NHAT HANH

It turned out that the round-trip to Kazantzakis's home was almost twenty kilometers instead of three. It had been a memorable day but a grueling one, and so after a nap and a shower I wandered the short distance from the Regal to Aegina's port. I decided to have dinner at the same restaurant that I had visited the previous night, Panta Rei. It was a block away from the water and the hubbub of the portside nightlife. Yesterday I had had one of the best meals of my life, and I was ready for another one. The dining room was dark-paneled, cool, and quiet. It was decorated with walnut picture frames that held quotations printed and drawn in Greek and English. Many of the frames held names and passages that I recognized from my study of philosophy and the classics. Ancient wisdom was repackaged and presented to a modern age. I sat at the polished bar and ordered a dinner of leeks and spinach baked in phyllo. The bartender didn't speak much English, so we communicated by pointing at the menu and nodding. I drank a couple bottles of Fix beer (which was almost as good as Mythos) and thought about my journey around the coastline.

Several of the framed quotations were in Greek without any English translation. I could figure out some of the names of the authors, but I didn't know enough Greek to read the passages themselves. The bartender did mention one Greek name that I could recognize: Heraclitus. I didn't know why the bartender mentioned him, and I couldn't learn much from the restaurant's framed quotes because most of them were in Greek and no one there could translate them for me.

I was also curious about the restaurant's name—Panta Rei. Most restaurants were named after places or persons, but this name seemed different, and I wondered what it meant. I knew enough Greek to ask the bartender that question, but he didn't know enough English to answer it. I decided to look it up when I got back to my hotel room and shrugged my shoulders, closing the conversation with a smile. The bartender smiled back and poured me a complimentary shot of something dark and sweet. When I paid the bill, he acknowledged his tip by hitting his chest twice with a closed fist, like a Roman gladiator.

When I did my research back in my hotel room, I discovered that Heraclitus was a monumental figure in the history of human thought. He had lived over a century before Socrates, around 500 BC, and thus he was categorized as one of the so-called pre-Socratic philosophers. The pre-Socratics were very early thinkers who struggled to make sense of the world and to plumb the fundamental basics of reality. What is the universe made of? How did existence originate? Very deep stuff, very vague, very subtle. Like the other pre-Socratic philosophers, Heraclitus speculated about the fundamental nature of the universe, especially the differences between *constancy* and *change*. He was fascinated with the basic ideas of *being* and *becoming*. He explored this intellectual territory about 2,500 years ago on the coast of Asia Minor, the land we now call Turkey. That's where my favorite island restaurant got its name and thereby taught me the lesson that closes this chapter and this book.

One of the fiercest debates between pre-Socratic philosophers raged between those who thought that the universe was in a constant state of change and those who believed that the appearance of change was nothing but an illusion. If this seems like a slightly ridiculous thing for intelligent adults to argue about, remember that human beings had just begun trying to explain the world *logically* and even *scientifically*. Before Heraclitus and his contemporaries, people had looked for answers to fundamental questions in myths about supernatural monsters, in legends about gods and heroes, and in folk tales and superstitions. The transition from the mythological way of explaining the universe to the rational examination of ideas and the natural world, even as it applied to such simple ideas as being and becoming, was a monumental step forward in human history. Some historians consider that transition to be the single most important event in the history of mankind.

Some of those pre-Socratic philosophers thought that the world constantly remained the same. Day after day, year after year, nothing ever changed. You think things are changing? You think that the present is becoming the future? Nope. Wrong. That's just the world playing tricks on you. It's sort of a cosmic optical illusion. Nothing actually ever changes; everything stays the same.

One of the leaders of that school of thought was named Parmenides. He believed that it was silly to think about things changing, because in order to do that, we would have to think about things that didn't even exist—at least not yet. After all, if the world is changing, Parmenides reasoned, what was it changing *into*? It must be changing into something new. Something different. Something that doesn't already exist. And thinking about something that doesn't exist is, as far as Parmenides was concerned, not just silly: it's *impossible*. Remember our discussion of goal-setting? One of the reasons that goals can't affect our present circumstances is because they require us to imagine and wish for things that do not exist and which, maybe, never will. Parmenides is famous, at least among people who study the history of philosophy, for saying, "We can speak and think only of what exists." Pretending that our wishes and our words can shape the future was, as far as Parmenides was concerned, a lot of nonsense.

Heraclitus, the guy my bartender mentioned, wasn't a wish-making, goal-setting fortune teller, but he did believe in change. To Heraclitus everything could change, would change, was changing, and would always keep changing. The world and everything in it—trees and plants, clouds and rain, stones and mountains and rocks and the land itself, and (here's the best part) even you and me—is constantly changing. Heraclitus said that nothing *could* stay the same. Changing into something else, becoming something that didn't yet exist, these developments were not simply possible, they were inevitable. We didn't have to predict the future or imagine a world that didn't exist to understand that. We only had to look around at the resolutions that the world was making right now. The universal resolve for change was knit into the fabric of everything.

Heraclitus believed that our senses tricked us into seeing constancy when, in fact, everything around us was already constantly changing. Remember Sartre's two waiters and the rule that existence precedes essence? I believe Heraclitus would have agreed with Sartre. Everything that exists must constantly express and create its essential self. Heraclitus's best-known explanation for this phenomenon is the example of a river. If you stand next to a river it might seem to you that the river is a natural constant. It has existed for thousands and thousands of years and it may last a million more. We can find it on a map that was drawn a hundred years ago and on a satellite image from right now. It seems to all the world as if the river that exists right now has always existed. The essence of The-River-of-Today has never changed.

But Heraclitus thought that it was this perception of constancy that was actually the cosmic optical illusion, and he demonstrated his conclusion with a thought experiment of his own. Imagine that one day you step off the riverbank and wade into the river. You will feel the water flowing past you. It may move quickly or slowly but it does move, and if you come back to the river tomorrow and step into it again, you will be feeling different water. The water from the first day has flowed downstream, and you are now standing in new water. The water you are wading in has changed. Even the riverbed, the sand, and the rocks that you step on will have moved and shifted at least a little. More change. Fish? Algae? Bubbles? Litter and floating trash? Change, change, change, change, and more change. The river you stepped in yesterday has become the *different* river that you stepped in today. It looks the same, but its essence has changed. Heraclitus explained this simple fact with one of the best-known epigrams in the history of philosophy:

"A person cannot step into the same river twice."

When you think about it, that makes perfect sense. But Heraclitus also knew that it wasn't just the river's essence that had changed since yesterday. The reason that a person cannot step into the same river twice is not just because the river has changed. *The person's essence has changed as well. You* have changed, too. Your existence has been altered; it has grown with every new experience. You may have learned some new things. You have certainly seen things, heard things, done things, and been exposed to things that have changed you in a thousand ways—some of which may be so imperceptible that you don't feel them. And so you think about yourself as if you remain unchanged, in just the same way that you once thought that about the river.

But you are not unchanged. You are never unchanged. The flow of your existence constantly produces a new personal essence, just as the flow of water constantly produces a new river. Some of your existential changes are small, but just as the flow of water can erode the river's banks and change its course, the tiny changes that make up the persistent flow of your personal existence produce a new essence in a life that has been forever changed. Forever transformed. Evolution. Renaissance.

The challenge we all face is governing the direction of that change. Do we move from good to better or from bad to worse? Do we fall asleep in our train car and ride along aimlessly, or do we dare to pull the Emergency Stop switch? Do we stay safe and static in the settlements to the east, or do we venture into the uncertain opportunities that lay beyond the frontier? These are the questions that we all must answer, like it or not. We are, as Sartre reminds us, condemned to be free; we have no choice. That means that we will either ride *The Imaginary Train* into obscurity or we will strike out on our personal existential journey to Renaissance. Heraclitus knew this, and if you think about it honestly for a minute, so do you. There is no such thing as standing still. Change is an inherent condition of all existence. Everything changes. Thousands of years ago, Heraclitus expressed this fundamental law of human existence with two words:

"Everything flows."

In Greek, "Everything flows" is "Panta rei"—and that is why my bartender mentioned Heraclitus and that is how my favorite restaurant got its name.

I went to Greece to write a book about living a changed life, and I ended up on a tiny island in a cozy little restaurant that was named for the very idea of becoming someone new. Weird, huh? Maybe so. But now, the best I can do is leave you with the wizard insight that a genius Greek discovered 2,500 years ago.

Panta rei. Everything flows, and so do we. In that we are all the same.

FOURTEENTH GUIDEPOST

We are changing and becoming new each and every day.
Recognize change.
Get used to it. Master it.

PART FIVE

Epilogue

"At the frontier, the bonds of custom are broken and unrestraint is triumphant.... In spite of environment, and in spite of custom, each frontier did indeed furnish a new field of opportunity, a gate of escape from the bondage of the past; and freshness, and confidence.... Impatience of its restraints and its ideas, and indifference to its lessons, have accompanied the frontier. What the Mediterranean Sea was to the Greeks, breaking the bond of custom, offering new experiences, calling out new institutions and activities, that, and more, the ever retreating frontier has been...."

FREDERICK JACKSON TURNER

The Imaginary Train

You keep watching the rider who has gotten off her train.

You don't know how old she is, but you know that once she was a child. And you know that like every child she had dreamed dreams about how her life would be when she grew up, and that most of those dreams did not come true. She had stretched out her hand to grasp the universe, but it had slipped between her fingers and skittered out of her imagination. Ever since she first learned about disappointment she has been scaling down her aspirations, dreaming of lesser miracles, hoping for smaller wonders, hungering for an opulent feast at life's table but learning to satisfy herself with skimpy leftovers and then with crumbs. You know that for her, "the whole wide world and all that's in it" soon shrank into a small house or apartment that she has no memory of picking out for herself. Eventually, that house or apartment and the universe it once had been was nothing more than a window seat on a rushing train. The world she once dreamed of holding in her hand roared past her—tantalizingly close, outside a speeding windowpane that gave her a blurry glimpse of reality shadowed by the reflection of the face she became when she learned how to stop dreaming.

She is walking toward you now. Each step is bouncier than the last one, and pretty soon she is close enough that you can hear what she is saying. "Where are we?" You are glad that she has walked in your direction and that she has asked for your help.

While she was still sitting in her window seat, there was no way for you to help her. You couldn't reach into that car and pull the switch for her. That was the part she had to do by herself.

But now that she is out here with you, there is a lot she needs to know, and you can be her teacher. After all, you got off the train first.

CHAPTER 15

FAREWELL

"He who postpones the hour of living
is like the rustic who waits for the
river to run out before he crosses."

HORACE

As our conversation draws to a close, I hope that you can see that, while you are different from everyone else in the world, we all share the commonality of being human. You were once a child. You had dreams, and many of those dreams slipped your grasp. You have been disappointed, and you have learned that failure is bitter for a long time while success may be sweet only briefly. You were taught to replace monumental unfulfilled dreams with modestly possible aspirations, and those aspirations have served you well. So far. They helped you build a safe and comfortable life for yourself, but it was incomplete and now it just isn't enough. Stopping your train may be hard and scary, but one thing is certain. No one can stop that train but you. You have to do that much alone. You are the only one who can pull the switch on artificiality and stop the conveyance that carries you past your real life. That one act, that one decision, will command the universe to come back to you so that you can try again to clasp on to it—this time with the sure and steady hands of an adult and not the dreamy fingers of a child.

If you are reading these words, that means that I finished writing this book, got it published, and somehow it found its way into your hands. Maybe someday I will write another one, and you will read that one, too. Maybe someday I will meet you at a bookstore or a signing party or a public speaking engagement. Maybe you will ask me a question and I will answer it, and the answer will mean something to you and you'll never forget it. Maybe. But maybe not. These may be the last words I ever share with you. From time to time we all face sad reminders that life is fleeting, irredeemable, and unpredictable. For me, today was such a time.

As I sat down to write this chapter, I received the awful news that a young friend had died this morning. Suddenly and without warning. He had not been sick or injured; there was no accident or violence. He just went to sleep last night and didn't wake up. I knew his father, who had died years ago, and so over the years I shared my memories of the father with the son. We didn't have the sort of friendship that kept us in contact every day, but we were both lawyers and we were always glad to run into each other and have time for a chat. He left behind a daughter and a wife whom, I shudder to imagine, must have awakened next to him in death this morning. I took my dog for a long walk today and tried to figure out what kind of world this is where healthy young fathers die in their sleep. And then I sat down to write a few of the things that I feel we should all remember. After all, who knows if we will ever meet again?

Farewell

This world where bad things happen is the same world where marvelous things happen, and some of those marvelous things are going to happen today and some of them are going to happen to you. You are going to take a breath and then take another one. You will have a heart that beats, and you will have someone somewhere who cares about you. Somewhere there is something worth doing that is waiting for you to do it. All of that means that you must live a life in full *today*.

Put off no good deed. Use your energy to be valuable and decent. Cast aside grudges. Begin great endeavors. Finish everything important. Nurture this moment. And then this one. And the next one. Speak the truth to others and especially to yourself. Make haste to be alive. Become a person who says, "Of course," to each worthwhile "Why not?" Remember to decide what your final words must not be and begin today to live the life that forbids them. Be aware that we have no warrant of tomorrow.

Strive mightily. Fail spectacularly. Then succeed wonderfully and start all over again. Keep no dream undreamt and let no important words remain unsaid. Take chances. Have adventures. Teach passionately. Learn voraciously. Risk fearlessly. Dare greatly. Forgive constantly. Believe in whatever you want to, but always in yourself. Search for wonders and discover them. Be prodigious in your appetite for amazement and swallow it whole. Let nothing escape you. Don't waste another instant looking at the world through a window that has your face spread across it in a fuzzy blur.

Conquer your frontier. Create your Renaissance.

If I can do it, so can you. No kidding.

Is today a good day to change your world?

Of course.

ABOUT
SPERO T. LAPPAS

Dr. Spero T. Lappas is an author, educator, lawyer, and artist headquartered in Harrisburg, Pennsylvania.

He was among the nation's youngest attorneys to be named in the first edition of *The Best Lawyers in America* and was later recognized in *Who's Who in American Law*, *Who's Who in the World*, *Who's Who in America*, *America's Leading Lawyers*, and *The Bar Register of Pre-Eminent Lawyers*. He served as lead counsel in hundreds of major cases, including some of Central Pennsylvania's most important trials.

He received the Doctor of Philosophy (American Studies) from the Pennsylvania State University where he was a University Graduate Fellow, the Juris Doctor (cum laude) from the Dickinson School of Law where he was a member of the

Editorial Board of the *Dickinson Law Review* and the National Trial Moot Court Team, and the Bachelor of Arts (cum laude) from Allegheny College. At Dickinson, he won two American Jurisprudence Awards and was later named to the Woolsack Society. At Allegheny, he was twice named an Alden Scholar; he received Departmental Honors at graduation, and won the Muhlfinger Prize for his independent research.

He served on the state advisory committees to study the causes of wrongful convictions and Pennsylvania's death penalty, as well as numerous directors' boards of private and non-profit organizations. He has also held faculty positions at Penn State, the Widener University School of Law, Messiah College, and Harrisburg Area Community College.

He is a frequent academic guest lecturer, legal educator, and community speaker. A prize-winning photographer, his artistic work has appeared in many solo exhibits, as well as in gallery shows, charity auctions, and private and corporate collections.

His earlier publications have appeared in *Dickinson Law Review, The Champion* (the journal of the National Association of Criminal Defense Lawyers), the Harrisburg *Patriot-News* (including a tenure as community columnist), *The Burg, The Pennsylvania Magazine of History and Biography,* and *The Encyclopedia of American Studies.* He co-authored "The Rocky Road to Reform: The Pennsylvania Experience," a chapter in *Wrongful Convictions and Miscarriages of Justice: Causes and Remedies in North American and European Criminal Justice Systems,* and contributed to *The Encyclopedia of American Studies* and *Youth Cultures in America.*

He has two children, Dr. Thom Lappas and Attorney Alexandria Lappas, and one grandchild, Spero Edward Lappas.

Conquer Life's Frontiers is his first book.